HOW TO
DESIGN & REMODEL
KITCHENS

DEUX

Created and designed
by the editorial staff
of ORTHO Books

Project Editor	Anne Coolman
Writer	Jenepher Walker
Designer	Jacqueline Jones
Illustrator	Rik Olson
Photographer	Stephen Marley
Photographic Stylist	Sara Slavin
Plan Designs	Diane Snow Crocker

Ortho Books

Publisher
Robert L. Iacopi

Editorial Director
Min S. Yee

Managing Editors
Anne Coolman
Michael D. Smith
Sally W. Smith

Production Manager
Ernie S. Tasaki

Editors
Jim Beley
Susan Lammers
Deni Stein

Design Coordinator
Darcie S. Furlan

System Managers
Christopher Banks
Mark Zielinski

Photographic Director
Alan Copeland

Photographers
Laurie A. Black
Richard A. Christman

Production Editors
Linda Bouchard
Alice Mace
Kate O'Keeffe

Asst. System Manager
William F. Yusavage

Chief Copy Editor
Rebecca Pepper

Photo Editors
Anne Dickson-Pederson
Pam Peirce

National Sales Manager
Garry P. Wellman

Sales Associate
Susan B. Boyle

Operations Director
William T. Pletcher

Operations Assistant
Gail L. Davis

Administrative Assistant
Georgiann Wright

Address all inquiries to
Ortho Books
Chevron Chemical Company
Consumer Products Division
575 Market Street
San Francisco, CA 94105

First Printing in April 1982

                    7 8 9
        87 88 89

ISBN 0-917102-98-3

Library of Congress Catalog Card
Number 81-86179

Chevron
Chevron Chemical Company
575 Market Street, San Francisco, CA 94105

Front Cover

Friendly and inviting, this sunny room welcomes the whole family, day or night. Its sparkling, white tile counters provide easy-to-clean light-reflecting surfaces, while the light oak warms up the room. Every type of work area is well defined, including a pastry and candy marble surface, reachable from both sides of the peninsula. Convenient cabinet storage hides all the necessary equipment and food, while open shelves house the everyday dishes that rotate regularly. For additional photographs of this kitchen, see pages 18 and 19.

Page 1

This inviting nook is a far cry from the formerly dismal corner of a mostly dark-brown kitchen. Writer Jenepher Walker and her husband, Paul Smith, use this area for eating, menu planning, reading the newspapers, paying bills, and playing dominoes. For a look at the "before" kitchen, see page 13, and then look at the results of their remodeling project on pages 94 and 95.

Back Cover

This bright, cheerful window area creates the feeling of cooking in a garden, with blooming flowers at counter height all year round. The stained-glass units—found at the outset of the remodeling project—became the focal point of the design. An efficient U-shape plan places the refrigerator, oven, and cooktop along the right wall, the sink at the outer wall, and a counter/pass-through on the left wall with storage cabinets above. Cabinet designs tie in with the charm of an older home, which is enhanced by the addition of an old, well-used chopping block as a central island for food preparation.

Acknowledgments

See page 96

HOW TO DESIGN & REMODEL KITCHENS

GETTING STARTED

Your kitchen remodeling begins
with what you already have.
Use the Kitchen Survey to assess
your needs and establish your priorities.
Then, using the sample Existing Plan
as a guide, translate your three-dimensional
space into a two-dimensional drawing.

If you are like millions of homeowners, you spend more time in your kitchen than anywhere else in your home. So it's probably important to you to have an attractive room as well as an efficient work space for preparing food. Creating such a kitchen is what this book is all about.

Maybe you are trying to work within a kitchen planned for an earlier age. You might be running yourself ragged in a large kitchen or cramped into a small postwar tract kitchen with out-of-date and inconvenient appliances. Or, perhaps your kitchen works fairly well but needs improved lighting or energy-saving appliances. Whatever your situation, you have probably already said to yourself, "Something has to be done." The next steps center around how far you can go, how much it will cost, what skills you will need, and where you can go for help.

Your budget may rule out total renovation plans, but "remodeling" can mean nothing more than adding a few shelves and applying fresh paint finishes. Or it can mean something more substantial, requiring carpentry, plumbing, and wiring skills. Although remodeling a kitchen is not a project to undertake lightly, you will find that everything falls into place if you take your time and break the project down into several steps. If you do not have basic skills, do some smaller projects first, and get help from friends and neighbors to upgrade your knowledge of building techniques.

As you start gathering kitchen ideas, consider an open design like this one. Family sitting and eating areas are well separated from kitchen activities, but the open room encourages relaxed gatherings. Harmonizing with the character of the old house, the colors, formal cabinetry, textures, and trim are all integral parts of a cohesive design. For other views of this kitchen, see pages 32 and 33.

The Book's Plan

Each chapter in this book covers one of the five stages in a remodeling project. The chapters are ordered in the sequence you should follow:

1. Getting started. Analyze the reasons for wanting to remodel by making a survey of your existing kitchen. Take a good, hard look at what you have now. Then draw a plan of your existing space. This will be the foundation for your new design. Chapter One provides guidelines for these two steps.

2. Defining your style. Chapter Two outlines the design process and provides a photographic tour of remodeled kitchens. By looking at a wide variety of kitchen styles, you develop a clearer sense of what you want to do in your own kitchen.

3. Creating a new design. Chapter Three shows you how to draw floor plans and elevation sketches for your new kitchen to help you develop your design through stages until you have just what you want. The Shopping Guide on pages 52 to 57 describes some of the products you will find on the market and prepares you for decisions you will need to make when selecting cabinets, appliances, and materials. Finally, this chapter helps you organize your project and estimate the time, money, and materials it may require.

4. Taking out the old. Chapter Four provides specific information on removing appliances and cabinets and on stripping walls and floors. By following the step-by-step instructions and diagrams, you should be able to do most of this work yourself.

5. Installing the new. Chapter Five outlines procedures for installing cabinets, hooking up new appliances and lighting, installing counter tops, laying new floors, and adding the finishing touches.

If you start at the beginning and work your way through, you will arrive at the end with a new kitchen that suits your needs and reflects your own style.

THE PROJECT OVERVIEW

At the beginning of any major project it helps to be cognizant of the basic issues that will affect you as you proceed. It would be wasted effort to plan a kitchen that your building department, budget, or schedule won't allow you to realize.

Building Permits

A visit to your local planning or building department will help you learn both the limitations and the possibilities of a remodeling project on your lot. In most communities there are restrictions on how far out you can build, how high up you can go, and what you can do without obtaining approval from your neighbors. You will need to know these basic facts before you can begin to consider your options.

Although there may be no restrictions on the types of alterations you wish to make, your building department usually requires you to obtain a permit for the construction. Whether or not you need a permit may depend on the total cost of your project, the degree of alteration, or both. If you need a permit, you will also be required to submit detailed working drawings showing any structural, plumbing, and wiring work you intend to do. If you plan to use a general contractor for the work, you may be able to rely on him to get the permit for you.

You will also need to know which codes cover which aspects of the construction so you will be able to meet the various building inspections as they occur. They generally come after rough plumbing is in, after rough electrical work has been done, after you have nailed up your wallboard, and after the subflooring is nailed down. A final inspection will be made after everything is hooked up and ready to go. You will not want to redo any work, so you should know how to do it correctly before you start. The individual inspectors can provide help and advice as you go along.

Money

Your bank and savings and loan offices are obvious sources of information on how to obtain the best possible financing for the size of your project. You may need only a higher limit on your credit card in order to purchase the necessary materials or a small personal loan to be paid back over a short time. For more extensive remodeling you may need a home improvement loan, a loan on the equity you have built up in the house, or even a refinancing arrangement on the house itself. It is also possible to obtain credit through your contractor or cabinet dealer or to seek help from a credit union, finance company, or life insurance company.

If you put in active or passive solar systems, some of your outlay may be retrievable through federal or state income tax deductions or credits. You will want to explore all possibilities before you get into the actual work.

When you work with professionals, give them a definite limit to the amount you can spend. However, it is all too easy to run a project over the originally intended budget limit. So don't start with your total figure during discussions. Pick a lesser amount.

Time

The amount of time you plan to devote to the project will include any tasks you take on personally, the days given to waiting for deliveries, and making followup calls to suppliers, picking up supplies, and cleaning up. If you are employed full time, you will have only evenings, weekends, and vacations. If the project is not extensive, this can be done. A very small kitchen can be taken apart and put back into working order over a weekend, with only a few more days needed for finishing up. New construction, alterations to the structure, and relocating appliances will take longer, in which case you may decide to leave the coordinating to a professional and just turn over the key.

If you are like many homeowners, you will do some work yourself and subcontract some of it. Perhaps you'll get involved in the dismantling process, have the professional supervise the major construction and installation, and then step in yourself to finish the room. This last stage can take as long as you can stand living in an unfinished kitchen. Most homeowners have found that remodeling takes far longer than they originally bargained for, so give this part of the planning some careful thought. Both schedules and budgets are discussed in more detail on pages 58 to 63. With these basic considerations in mind, move on to phase one of your project.

Gathering Ideas

Start your project with one of the most enjoyable aspects: gathering ideas. There are many sources to which you can turn.

Magazines. If you have not already loaded up your supermarket cart with magazines, do so. "Shelter" publications, which deal with the home and its design, are full of innovative plans and new ways to use materials and products. The ads represent the newest and best of the products currently on the market. There are also special interest magazines devoted to kitchens. These contain just about all the products, manufacturers, and information you need to get started on your own collection of ideas.

Trade publications. If you have access to a large public library or the office of an architect or a contractor, look over some of the magazines distributed only to the trade. Some manufacturers, such as hardware producers, advertise only to the trade, and you will not get to see their products anywhere else.

Manufacturers. In most ads, the manufacturer provides some method for obtaining further information. The in-

Start a clipping file of kitchen photographs that spark ideas you might want to try. In the kitchen shown here (and on page 38), open shelves above a breakfast counter let in daylight and do not obstruct the view of the dining room; yet they retain valuable storage space and provide an eye-catching display space. For more ideas see Chapter Two, which begins on page 17.

formation includes brochures, many of them in color; specification sheets that give actual dimensions and finishes for the various lines of products; pamphlets that instruct you on how to install certain elements; and lists of dealers in your general area. If the product advertised is a big-ticket item, the manufacturer may alert your local retailer to your interest and you may be invited to look over the showroom displays.

Check your local library for *Sweet's Catalog.* This is a compilation of many brochures put together for architects, designers, and builders. It contains hundreds of photographs and illustrations arranged by topic and manufacturer that can give you additional ideas about how to select and install products in your own kitchen design.

Professional and trade associations. Manufacturers and professionals belong to associations that often provide lists of local dealer sources and materials. They may also produce informative booklets on how kitchen cabinets are made, how to install ceramic tiles, or how to work with a kitchen designer. Most will not recommend individual manufacturers, suppliers, or professionals, but they can be of help in answering your general questions.

Showrooms. One of the best ways to get hands-on knowledge about specific products that intrigue you is to visit the showrooms of kitchen specialists, building suppliers, lumberyards, home improvement centers, plumbing suppliers, and other specialists. Although some outlets may sell only to contractors and other professionals, you can still look over an array of products that you might not find elsewhere. You can check out cabinet door hinges, the way drawers slide, and the final look of various finishes. You can turn on faucets to see whether they work easily and look over the styles to see just which spout works best with which faucets. You can open oven doors, measure different types of sinks, peer inside cabinets to see interior finishes and shelf adjustments, and read the control panels of major appliances. Catalogs and specifications are available, and you may be able to borrow sample chips or books to consider products more carefully at home. There you can see just how various materials will look under the actual day and night lighting of your own kitchen.

Organizing Your Research Materials

You will very quickly accumulate a pile of materials that you should organize to maintain a sense of order during your planning. File folders, scrapbooks, or three-ring notebooks with pockets are all helpful for grouping brochures, magazine pages, and notes. Separate them under such headings as Layout, Counter Tops, Appliances, Lighting, Cabinets, and so on. As you sort them into their various categories, the whirl of ideas circling around in your mind will begin to sort itself out.

Clip photos from brochures rather than keeping piles of dog-eared pamphlets. Jot down any dimensions necessary for planning, and put pamphlets dealing with installation aside during the planning stage. You can also winnow out those ideas and products you don't like.

While you're gathering new ideas and compiling your notebook, take a close look at what you already have. Even if you decide to go to a kitchen designer, architect, or contractor, you'll be asked to go through the same steps outlined in this chapter. So make the Kitchen Survey outlined on the following pages, possibly saving yourself some money. When the survey is completed, you will have a basic list of priorities that will help you keep on track throughout your project. This list and the Existing Plan of your kitchen (see pages 14–15) will be the foundation for all your future planning.

Start by thinking through the primary activities that take place in your kitchen—cooking, serving, eating, and cleaning up—and list the major problems that occur during each. Most of the questions in the following sections ultimately relate to how your kitchen works—or does not work—for you. By looking at your kitchen first in terms of activity "centers," you'll quickly pinpoint areas to which you should pay particular attention. Then create one page in your notebook for each of the following categories: Layout, Traffic Patterns, Counter Space, Cabinets and Other Storage Areas, Appliances, Surfaces, Lighting, and Style. Note special difficulties and needs under each heading. Try to determine what the biggest problem is and how it affects your kitchen activities. As you prepare your lists, possible alternatives or solutions may come to mind. That's fine. Make note of them for future reference. But don't focus on solutions right now; keep your attention on the very real drawbacks you currently face. The questions that follow will help you focus on the specific problems that are prompting you to take on this project in the first place. They are by no means exhaustive, but they should prompt other questions of your own, helping you determine your real priorities.

Basic Layout and Traffic Patterns

Kitchen planning experts all talk about the **work triangle** formed by the three major appliances—sink, stove, and refrigerator. Their arrangement determines the number of footsteps necessary for one person to prepare or clean up a meal. The recommended distances are 4 to 7 feet on each side of the triangle, totaling 12 to 22 feet for all three sides. For top efficiency, planners place the sink at an equal distance from the other two

corners of the triangle. It's not essential that your plan measure up to the norm, but by answering the following questions you may be able to determine some of the basic problems. For instance, do you walk too far between any two points of the triangle? Or are two of the points almost on top of each other? Further, how many cooks work in your kitchen? Do you bump into each other as you move around? Can you stand side by side at the cooking surface? Are you working around one another at the only sink? Is there a peninsula? Island? Worktable? Is there a place to eat? Are they all arranged for maximum efficiency? If not, list the problems.

Next, walk from the kitchen into the dining room, the laundry room, and the garage. Go back to the kitchen and make some notes: How many doors open into the room? Are they all necessary? Do kids and pets troop through your work space to get from one room to another? What happens when company comes and moves into the kitchen to help? Must you run around a corner to get to pantry items? Where are your laundry facilities? Would it make more sense to move them into or out of the kitchen? If you find you are doing more walking than working, go back to the assessment of your layout. Try to outline the major problems.

Counter Space

Counter space should function primarily as a work surface. Is this true in your kitchen? Or are the counters more like storage shelves? Are you trying to do all your kitchen tasks on one small counter? Do your kids draw or do homework at your serving counter? Do you have a place for dirty dishes near the sink? A drainboard for clean ones? A place to chop? A place to lay out dinner plates when serving food? Do you have space to put down large grocery bags next to the refrigerator? Is there room to sit a hot pot down next to the cooking surface or the oven? Are your counters all the same height? Can you sit at any of them? Are any approached from both sides? List the areas where your biggest problems occur, where you want more counter space or where you have counter space that isn't used efficiently.

Cabinets and Storage

Lack of storage space is often caused by cabinets that are full of items which rarely, if ever, get used. Before answering the questions listed below, note everything you have not used during the past year or have taken out

only once or twice. You may be able to find other places for these items. Then ask: Is there wasted space above the flat stacks of plates and bowls? Is there a cabinet wide enough to hold mixing bowls? Salad bowls? Mixer? Are cupboards too high to reach? Too low? Too shallow? Too deep? Is there space between the cupboard and the ceiling where dust accumulates? Are shelves adjustable? Do the tall vinegar and oil bottles fit? Are cooking utensils stored by the stove? How convenient are the drawers for flatware and table accessories? Do you have any pantry or other storage space large enough to hold the biggest roasting pan, large coffee urn, bags of cat or dog food, mop and broom, vacuum, or picnic baskets and coolers? When you've checked out every existing storage space, list both your problems and needs in terms of drawers, shelves, bins, closets and their desirable widths, depths, or heights. If the only thing wrong with the cabinets is the way they look, consider refinishing them or just changing the doors. However, your next consideration is the appliances, and if you change them you may be forced to alter your cabinetry.

Appliances

Sink. If you are replacing the counter, you may have to disconnect the sink, so decide whether you want to reinstall your existing one. Is it scratched or discolored? Is your sink too low, too high, too deep, too shallow? Do large items like grills or roasting pans fit into it? Can you fill large pots easily? Does the garbage get mixed up with utensils and dishes? Do you use the second sink or wish you had one? Does the nozzle swing wide enough and high enough? Before moving on to the second point of your work triangle, decide whether or not you like the location of your sink.

Range/Cooktop/Oven. Even if there is nothing wrong with the appliance, ask yourself whether it serves your needs adequately. Do you have gas and prefer electric or vice versa? Do you have enough burners? Are they big enough? Are the burners far enough apart to handle big pots or woks? Is the oven too small? Too slow? Could you use a microwave? Do you dislike your range enough to put it on your "must replace" list, or is the problem something else—a bad location, for example? List all the pros and cons about your current cooking appliances.

Refrigerator/Freezer. This is the third appliance in your work triangle. Does the door swing in the right direction? Is it reversible? Does it block anything or is it blocked by another appliance? Is the refrigerator big enough? Is the freezer big enough? How convenient is it to reach the ice? Is the appliance self-defrosting or do you have to defrost it? How often? Does it have energy-saving features? If your main problem is that you can't open the door wide enough to get the crispers fully open, perhaps you can save the cost of a new refrigerator merely by relocating the existing one. Or perhaps you can have it refinished to match a new color scheme. Decide whether or not replacing the refrigerator is a must.

Dishwasher. If you're moving the sink, the dishwasher may have to be relocated, too. Is this the time for a new one? Or a second one? How often do you use it? Does it have energy-saving cycles? Are the racks convenient for loading? Does it get the dishes really clean? Does it ever break down? How easy is it to have repaired? When open, does the door interfere with the traffic pattern or with other cabinet doors? Is it convenient to the sink and to cupboards where clean dishes go? Does loading and unloading disrupt the work and circulation in the kitchen?

Trash compactor. Assess how high on your priority list this appliance should go. Is it convenient? Do you empty it every couple of days? Would you spend more on garbage collection without it? If the answer to these questions is "no," reconsider your need for this appliance. The storage space it displaces may be more valuable to you.

Surfaces

Although many of your options for surfaces are related to style and color, you should consider the practical aspects: How often do you have to wax or clean your floor? Does it show dirt easily? Is it looking worn or dated in color or pattern? Is your plastic laminate counter burnt or scratched? Is the wood chopping block waterstained? How discolored is the grout between your tiles? Could the walls use a fresh coat of paint or some lively new wallpaper? Remember to consider all the major surfaces in relation to each other. If you replace one, you may want to replace others to maintain a particular look or style. Or you may be able to refinish the surface to update its look while saving some money.

THE KITCHEN SURVEY

Lighting

Notice how light affects the space in the morning, at noon, and at dusk. Is your kitchen too dark to work in without artificial light? Could you enlarge or add a window? Is there a shadowed area over the sink? Over the stove? Are the backs of the counters in darkness? Is it difficult to read the morning paper at the kitchen table or counter? Can fixtures be moved or turned? Exactly what is it about them that you don't like, other than design? Analyze your lighting in terms of general ambient lighting and lighting for specific tasks. List all the problems you find.

Style

Make a list of the existing style elements in your kitchen—colors, textures, cabinet style, and so on; then answer these questions: Do you like the basic look of your present kitchen? Does it have a particular style? If so, what is it? Do you like your present color scheme? Are there structural elements you want to disguise or emphasize? What about the details? Do all the handles or knobs match? Are they in keeping with the style of your cabinets? Where do you hang dish towels? Are they just hooked through the refrigerator door handle? Can you reach oven mitts when you stand in front of the oven? Are your pots hanging from large nails instead of hooks? Do you have room for an attractive rack? Note all the elements that contribute to the overall look of your kitchen and write down everything you like or dislike about the look of your kitchen.

Structure

Kitchen **walls** may be constructed of wallboard, plaster and lath, wood paneling, brick, stone, or adobe. If your tentative thinking calls for expansion, you'll want to know whether walls are load-bearing or not. Spotting the difference is tough—bearing and nonbearing walls look identical. If you have the original building plans, you will be able to tell. If not, a good rule of thumb is to see whether there is a wall either upstairs or downstairs in the identical position. If there is, chances are you are dealing with a bearing wall. If not, it is probably a partition wall. The difference is critical if you are considering tearing out a wall. A nonbearing wall is merely a partition and the only problem in removing it is clearing away the rubble and patching walls and floors. A load-bearing wall is part of the basic structure and, like the exterior walls, is used for support. If you remove such a wall, you will have to install a heavy beam to carry the load.

While looking at the walls, see whether or not outside walls have been insulated and whether they show signs of leaks or dampness. In an older house, check whether your framing is 2 by 6s rather than today's standard 2 by 4 studs. The wider studs, sometimes placed farther apart than the 16-inch norm now used, might make it harder to work with standard doors and windows. Some older houses have walls with no studs at all. They are constructed with tongue-and-groove boards attached either horizontally or vertically and serve to

wall off a smaller room. Such construction requires replacement or reinforcement if you plan to hang heavy objects like kitchen cabinets. The wood can be saved for use in a more decorative, visible way.

Determine whether **ceilings** are plasterboard, plaster over lath, panels on beams, acoustical tile suspended from a metal gridwork, or something else. Some of today's high style kitchens pictured in magazines feature interesting uses of the air space. To get additional height, you might want to go up into an attic or second floor space. Or you may have a high ceiling you'd like to lower in order to provide a more cozy feeling with a well-lit area beneath a grid of diffusers.

Check your **floors** for squeaks or slopes. If you're thinking of installing a number of additional heavy appliances, make sure your foundation and floors will carry the extra weight. You may need professional advice to be sure of this.

Plumbing

If you are considering rerouting appliances, familiarize yourself with the existing plumbing and with the way appliances work so you know what supply, drain, and vent lines are needed. Transferring your sink to the opposite counter may require all new venting as well as plumbing. Switching from an electric to a gas stove will entail running pipe to the gas supply. (Make sure you have one.) On the other hand, moving the refrigerator may be as simple as finding another outlet—unless you have an icemaker, which requires additional plumbing.

Trace all pipes and note the location of connections and shutoff valves. Note which are waste lines, which are supply lines, and which are hooked into the water heater. This step may prove difficult and will certainly entail crawling around in the basement or under the house and peering into the base cabinets. It may also require professional assistance. See Ortho's book, *Basic Plumbing Techniques*.

Wiring

The wiring systems in many older homes cannot carry the load of today's appliances. Certain appliances use a lot more electricity than others and require their own circuit with a grounded outlet. This is true of electric ranges and ovens—microwave or conventional. If you are adding appliances or relocating existing ones, you will have to provide heavy-duty outlets, which may mean doing some rewiring.

Check the capacity of your system at the point where the main line enters your service panel—it is usually in the basement, garage, or entryway. If your home is old and has a fuse box, chances are that you have 110-volt wiring instead of the 220-volt wiring required by today's appliances. Newer homes have circuit breakers that switch off automatically when any one line is overloaded.

Check which fuses or circuits serve which rooms by unscrewing fuses or flipping switches to cut off the power. When you have located the kitchen lines, turn the circuit breakers on and off again to see which lines serve what. Some outlets or switches may be on the same line, and some may be on separate lines. Those on separate lines may be capable of powering additional fixtures.

If there are blanks in the service panel, you may already have additional lines available. If you need more power, the utility company will have to install new lines. In order to complete your assessment of the wiring, you may want to use Ortho's book, *Basic Wiring Techniques,* or seek professional assistance.

Heating and Cooling

If you are satisfied with your heating and cooling systems, just note the location of motor, ducts, and outlets. If you are not satisfied with your systems and will be opening up walls to expose and do plumbing work, now is the time to make changes. You'll need to know exactly what you have before you can decide on possible changes.

In a steam or hot water system where heat is distributed through a loop system of pipes, you can tap in an additional radiator. You may wish to relocate air ducts for a gravity or forced-air heating system. A more convenient place for a duct might be under the kitchen sink, with a grill in the toekick (the recess at the bottom of base cabinets). That way, you'd have the warm air coming into the kitchen at a point where it would warm you more efficiently and be out of the way as well.

Now would also be the time to consider how you can lower your heating costs. For more information on this subject, see Ortho's book, *Energy-Saving Projects for the Home.* Any air conditioners directed into the present space should be examined for efficiency. Perhaps they need only insulation around the ducts. Or perhaps better window venting would enable them to work fewer hours during hot weather.

Survey Review

When you have enumerated the problems in your present kitchen, examined its structure, and scrutinized all the mechanical systems, organize your priorities. Go over all your notes. In each area, make a list of the most important things that are in need of change. Pull these together and make a "must change" list of top priorities.

Then look at your notes again for less critical problem areas. Make a list of these lesser priorities and label it "would like to change." The rest of the items on your lists will be those that would be nice to change if at all possible, or that are okay now and not in need of change. When your priorities are listed and firmly in mind, you should be able to focus on your most important changes, even when you are dazzled by items beyond your budget.

The Kitchen Survey will help you define the functional and style elements you want in your new design. Here, well planned storage units and a simple color scheme makes cooking both efficient and pleasant. For another view turn to page 16.

YOUR EXISTING PLAN

When you have completed your priority list, put it aside for a bit so you can draw your Existing Plan which is an exact, two-dimensional rendering of your kitchen as it is right now. It will form the basis for all your future planning. First measure the overall dimensions of your kitchen (including any additional closet or other space that you might use) and the elements in the kitchen that you may keep. To make this plan, you'll need some inexpensive materials that are easy to find in hardware, stationery, or art supply stores:

- ☐ retractable steel tape
- ☐ ruler, 18 inches long
- ☐ graph paper (four or eight squares to the inch—¼- or ½-inch squares)
- ☐ pencils
- ☐ eraser
- ☐ tracing paper
- ☐ masking tape
- ☐ plastic template of kitchen elements
- ☐ plastic triangle
- ☐ compass

You can do all your measuring first and mark the measurements on a rough sketch of your kitchen, or measure and draw to scale as you go. If your paper has a ½-inch scale, use one square for every foot. If your paper has a ¼-inch scale, use two squares for every foot.

Floor Plan

The most important part of your Existing Plan will be a scale drawing showing the floor plan of your kitchen, including cabinets and storage areas; cooktop, refrigerator, and sink; work and eating areas; the hot water heater, air conditioner, and other mechanical devices; and electrical and plumbing lines. The following sections outline the steps you must take in order to prepare a detailed floor plan.

Perimeter. Measure the basic width and length of the kitchen plus any adjacent areas you might use. Measure the distance of doors and windows from a corner or the end of a wall and from each other. Measure the width of their moldings or trims. Draw a line for each wall, leaving the proper amount of space for each door or window. Draw a second line outside the first. These parallel lines indicate a normal 4-inch wall. Fill in the space between the two lines with solid penciling.

Next, draw in the doors. If a door swings, show it in the open position. Using a compass spread to the width of the door, make a quarter circle from the hinges. Make a semicircle if the door swings both ways. For sliding doors, draw in the fixed one, and then indicate whether the sliding one is inside or outside the fixed one, and show it about halfway open. For folding doors, show a series of little w's to the depth of each panel. Show pocket doors half open, sitting within the stud wall pock-

ets. Draw in the windows. Use a compass to show the way they swing or use the half-open position for sliding windows.

Base cabinets. Measure these individually, as a whole bank of units, or both. Measure both width and depth, front to back. (Base cabinets in older homes are often shallower than today's standard 24-inch depth.) Measure door and drawer widths as well so you can compare them to new modules you may want to install. Draw in one long line to show the counter edge of a wall of units, three lines for a peninsula, and all four edges for an island.

Next, draw in the sink opening and the cooktop on the counter top outline, using either your template or measurements you make yourself. If you think you may want to keep them in their current locations, measure the width and depth of the range, refrigerator, dishwasher, and laundry appliances and plot them on your scale drawing.

Wall cabinets. These are normally 12 inches deep, compared to 24-inch base cabinets. Measure these units individually, as a whole bank, or both, just as you did the base units. While you are working along the upper bank of cabinets, measure wall vents or hoods that are attached to them. Draw the upper cabinets on your plan with a dashed line to show the proper distance back from the front counter edge of the base unit. Draw in one long dashed line to indicate a whole bank of units. Then draw in their door swings with dashed lines, showing how they swing out into the counter and the head area. If the hood over the range or any other cabinets project out farther than the standard 12-inch depth, indicate that on the plan.

Storage or pantry areas. Measure the width and depth of each storage or pantry area. Draw them in the same way you drew in base cabinets, but show that the counter top stops when it meets the pantry. Indicate how the pantry door swings.

Work areas. These are often a problem, so measure how many inches of counter space you have to the left and right of both the sink and the cooktop, and indicate

---

As noted at the beginning of this chapter, kitchen remodeling begins with what you have now. The two photographs to the right are "before" shots of a small corridor kitchen used throughout this book to illustrate the various steps in creating any new kitchen design. The photographs immediately pinpoint certain problems: the room's dark and cramped look, the clutter, and the conflicting shapes and patterns. You may feel you know your kitchen's faults all too well, yet photographs such as these help you see the room more objectively. And because you'll be using two-dimensional tools (floor plans and elevations) to create your new design, photographs help you make the transition from three dimensions to two. On the next two pages you'll find this same kitchen in plan form, which is the starting point for a new design.

these spaces on your plan. Note the dimensions of counter space by the refrigerator. If ovens are separate from the cooking area, measure the nearest space for putting down hot dishes.

Work triangle. If you have not already done so in your survey, measure your work triangle from cooktop to sink to refrigerator to cooktop again—midpoint to midpoint—and indicate these measurements in another color somewhere on your plan or on a tissue overlay.

Eating areas. Whether eating areas are built in or not, measure them precisely. Note the size of chairs and stools—side to side and front to back—and how much clearance you need for pushing them back or getting your knees under the table or counter. Note the size of any tables and the size of their pedestals or bases.

Other elements. Measure and draw in floor grills. Measure the hot water heater, furnace, air conditioner, and any other mechanical devices located within the kitchen area, and draw them in on your plan. If there is a door leading to their space, measure and draw in the length and direction of its swing. Note the location of all outlets, light switches, and light fixtures. Indicate where water and gas lines enter your kitchen. Note connections for an icemaker or island appliances.

When your heating units and utility lines are drawn in, you should have a complete floor plan in front of you, with all the elements that you may keep shown on the drawing. Sit back and look at it, darkening lines here and there if you need to clarify what's going on.

Elevations

After completing the floor plan of your kitchen, you will also find it helpful to make a similar scale drawing of each wall. These drawings, called elevations, provide a useful visual aid when you're generating new ideas. On a separate sheet of graph paper for each wall—call them north, south, east, and west—do exactly what you did for the floor area. Draw a plan of everything on that wall: base cabinets, wall cabinets, appliances, storage space, doors, windows, grills or vents, light fixtures, and outlets. Draw the room height to scale as well as the heights and widths of all other elements on the wall. Draw the frames around the windows and doors. If there is complicated molding and trim, merely draw the width to scale with straight lines. Position the windows and doors the right distances down from the ceiling and away from corners. When you draw the base cabinets, outline the doors and drawers. Don't bother with paneling, molding, or hardware unless you need some visual aids for the purpose of comparison to a new look. The same holds true for the upper cabinets. Draw in door and open-shelf outlines. Draw in appliances with just enough detail so you know what they are. Don't forget the hood across the top of the cooking area, pantry units or closet doors, pass-throughs, and eating counters. When the elevations are finished, you will have a complete set of drawings—a plan of your kitchen as it is now. You will use these drawings as the basis for new floor plans and elevations. The sketches on page 15 will give you an idea of what yours will look like.

YOUR EXISTING PLAN

Floor Plan

In the floor plan of the small, corridor kitchen pictured on page 13, various problem areas are shown in two dimensions. The narrow chopping block between the range and refrigerator presents an impossible work area, and hot pots cannot be placed on the wood. The overlapping range, refrigerator, and dishwasher doors become obvious, and the refrigerator blocks passage to the pantry. The trash compactor, which is already taking up valuable storage space, also blocks the entrance from the adjacent dining room when it is open. The electrical outlets are actually well spaced, with the only three-wire plug behind the range. One wall switch activates a hanging lamp over the eating area, and another controls both the single fixture in the work area and a short tube over the sink. A cold-water intake line is located in the pantry area behind the refrigerator. The sink and dishwasher work off the same hot-water supply lines, and the dishwasher drain is connected through an air gap to the disposal. The telephone jack next to the window has a long cord that leads to a phone on the counter, along with a clutter of note pads, pencils and other message-taking paraphernalia. Following this type of analysis in your own kitchen, pinpoint the areas that need your attention. When you begin to draw elevations, you'll have a good idea of your focus.

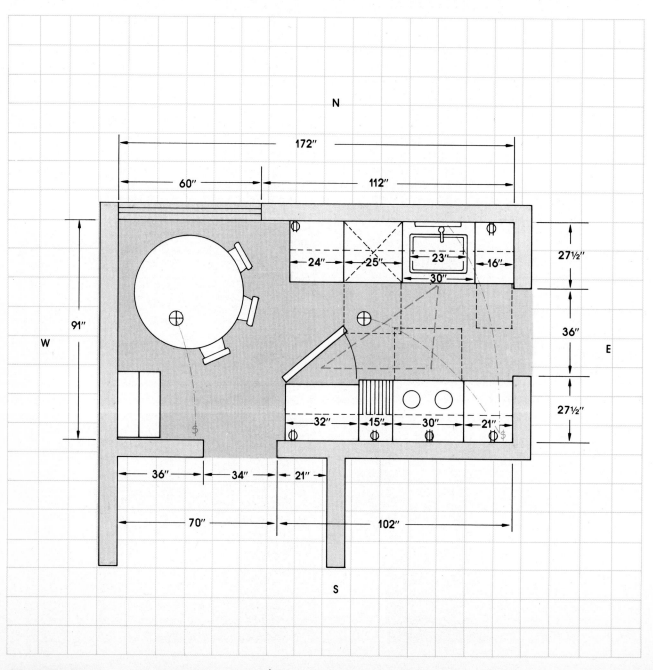

Elevations

Elevations for all four walls of this same kitchen are illustrated below. Not only do the narrow base and wall cabinets create cramped counter surfaces and crammed storage space, but they also have a ragged, uneven look. Further, the dark finish absorbs all available daylight and offsets the white of the appliances, making them appear even larger than they are. Door hinges, particularly above the dishwasher, are inconvenient for practical use. Even the design of the cabinet fronts—with raised panels that pull the eye inward—makes them appear smaller. All cabinet shelves are fixed, and none are high enough to store vases, bottles, or other tall items. Space above the wall cabinets tends to get used for storing bulky or extra items, which is impractical and looks messy. Spice racks over the sink are inconvenient for use and for preserving the spices—heat from the sink's steam and light from the fixture cause them to deteriorate quickly. The hutch at the end of the room, though needed for extra storage, cramps the round table. Dark shutters on the north wall let in little light even when tipped open. When you make these kinds of notations on your elevation sketches, and combine them with those you made during your Kitchen Survey, you have a very complete picture of the problems you'll want to solve in your new design.

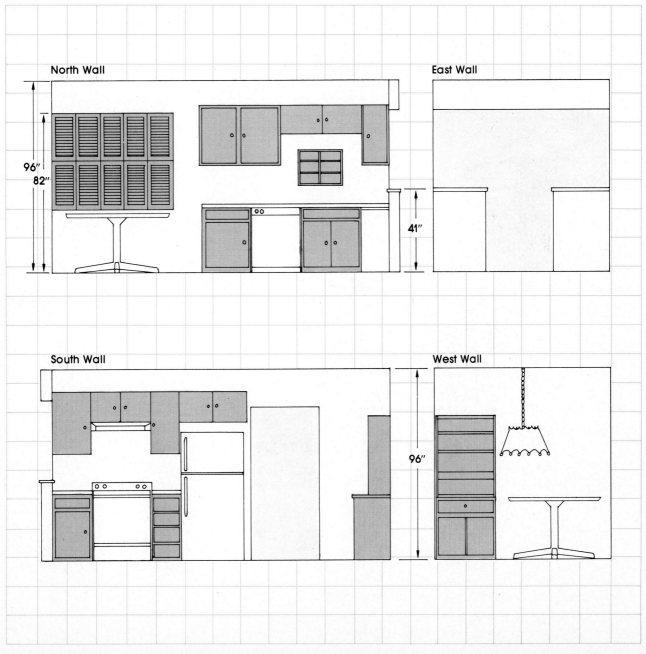

North Wall

East Wall

South Wall

West Wall

KITCHEN STYLES

Take this photographic tour of
others' kitchens to spark ideas for your own.
When you can define the feeling
you want your kitchen to have—
in pictures even more than in words—
you'll be ready to create your own new design.

Good kitchen design boils down to creating a plan that is functional and developing an overall design scheme that not only suits this function, but is also one you genuinely like. To create such a plan, you can follow some basic design procedures.

The Process of Design

Designing is a process that entails generating and expressing ideas for a particular situation—in this case, your kitchen—and you've already got a good start. You established your goals and priorities in the Kitchen Survey, and you outlined the givens of your existing kitchen by measuring and drawing your Existing Plan. The remaining stages of design are not mysterious, but they do not follow a straight path. They overlap and merge into one another. However, the same basic steps included in creating any new kitchen are listed here.

1. Define the look or style you like. Use the photos in this book and in your notebook, make visits to showrooms and model kitchens, and look over brochures. Pinpoint the elements used in kitchens you like and note how they have been tied together into an overall design scheme. Note various color combinations and the difference good lighting makes. See how hard and soft textures can affect the look. Study the differences that pattern makes in a room.

2. Start getting some ideas down on paper. Use the floor plan of your existing kitchen as a base, and decide where you'd like to locate your various activity centers, such as cooking, serving, eating, and cleaning up. Tie these centers together with counter spaces and storage units, paying close attention to traffic patterns and clusters of activities.

Strong architectural forms are the keynotes of this distinctive kitchen design. With its own square "windows" and double pass-through, the high end wall echoes the exterior window wall, the wood floor and ceiling help contain the room's massive volume, and the simple and efficient U-shape work space is tied into the overall design with wood trim.

3. When you're satisfied with a general layout, draw elevation sketches of each wall and figure out your ideal storage arrangement—cabinets, drawers, bins, closets, pull-out shelves, and so on. Then play with the horizontal and vertical lines these individual elements create in order to tie them together into a unified whole. And finally, try out ideas for color, light, patterns, and textures until you are satisfied with the overall look of the kitchen.

4. Create a preliminary list of the elements you will need to purchase. Shop around to see what products and materials are available that will meet your practical needs and suit your design scheme.

5. Estimate the cost of your project. Using your floor plans, elevation sketches, and shopping lists, make sure you're within your budget. If you plan to do all the work yourself, estimate the cost of your materials, tools, and supplies. If you intend to use professionals, get at least three bids. If you discover that you're over budget, adjust your plans accordingly.

6. Turn your plans into a working drawing. This final, detailed drawing, which may have to be approved by your local building department, will guide you or the professionals you hire through the physical work of remodeling, and from it you will draw up a list of products and materials you will actually purchase.

7. Establish a schedule. Plan the sequence of work, decide how long each process will take, who will do each task and when. Compare this schedule with your personal and business schedules so there will be no conflicts. Check delivery times on materials and fixtures you want, and make sure you order them or have them ordered far enough ahead of the time you will need them. Then write up contracts with any professionals you plan to hire.

With your working drawings, material lists, and schedule in hand, you'll be ready to translate your design into reality. Even if you're eager to get your new kitchen installed, don't rush the design. A big problem with many kitchen remodeling projects is poor planning, which leads to disappointment.

Define Your Style

When you begin designing your new kitchen, function will be your basic building block. You begin with layout, storage needs, traffic patterns, and so on. But if you also have some idea of the look you want your kitchen to have at the outset of your project, you'll know what elements to work with and what dimensions to use. If you want a comfortable, cozy kitchen with a round, pedestal table and ladder-back chairs, you will approach your layouts from one perspective. But if you want a sleek, efficient kitchen with a built-in counter for quick meals, you'll approach your layouts very differently. Therefore, with your priority list as a guide, you can define the style you'd like to achieve.

Style is commonly defined in terms of certain catch words like "traditional," "contemporary," "provincial," or "country." Sometimes such terms help you describe what you want, but at other times they may actually limit you. It is far more helpful to avoid the limitations of such terminology and define your style goals in pictures.

Look at the photographs on the following pages and throughout the book. They represent a wide range of kitchen styles and ideas. Some may appeal to you immediately, some may grow on you, and some may leave you completely cold. Rarely will a kitchen fall into a category that can be described with one term. Yet each one can help you define the feeling you want. Compare these photos to others you've been gathering. Visit stores and showrooms where kitchen models are on display, and pick up brochures. Make notes of everything you like, whether an entire kitchen or an oven mitt. As you consider all the possibilities, what appeals to you? An uncluttered look with everything out of sight? Smooth surfaces, light or dramatic colors, and simple, functional accessories? Or do you prefer a busy workshop with everything hanging on the walls and within reach? You may like dark-stained, carved cabinet doors with intricate hardware, or you might prefer natural woods with only a light wax and no hardware. Or wood beams, handmade tiles, stucco walls, and open shelves may be what catch your eye. As you plot each detail in your own design, you can refer to your collection of photos and notes to help you select elements that create this feeling and to help tie these elements together.

For a family whose whole life revolves around the kitchen, this warm, inviting room (shown on these two pages and on the front cover) provides a pleasant spot to work and gather.

Its clean lines present an uncluttered look with just a few open shelves and a sunny greenhouse window to lend some color and friendliness (far left). Medium wood tones add warmth without decreasing light, and work surfaces are light and slick, except for the large chopping block on the island that also serves as an eating bar. Oak cabinetry and appliance panels, tiled counters and backsplashes, a two-sided marble pastry slab on the end of a peninsula, and a cluster of easy-to-reach pots and pans all contribute to the design goals established by the family at the outset of their project. Even the sink counter has been planned to extend out into the new greenhouse space where plants are easy to water and tiles catch the drips from pots and hanging baskets. Open shelves have been installed in two places: beside the large refrigerator/freezer, where a collection of colorful hand-painted mugs and pitchers is displayed next to glasses and stemware, and directly over the dishwasher for everyday dishes, which rotate regularly and therefore do not collect dust.

To accommodate a six-burner range (above left) and still have landings for hot kettles to either side, the righthand counter is angled back toward the sink area. A second oven is built into the wall by the refrigerator (immediate left) with storage above and below, and the rear wall accommodates additional storage. Personal touches, like the rear-wall prints framed with colorful mattes, and the Italian hand-painted tiles over the range, add charm to what is an extremely functional kitchen.

Crisp, clean lines and pale colors visually push out the walls of this narrow kitchen and give the room a look of quiet and efficient order. Yet behind the flat-faced cabinets is a vast array of kitchen equipment and food used by a busy, professional gourmet cook. Pull-out shelves, drawers, and bins are all carefully planned to eliminate bothersome clutter.

The height of the ceiling is counterbalanced by the use of strong horizontal lines in the basic design, such as the wide cornice running over the cooking area (left), the steel-edged shelf above the range, and the open cookbook shelves at the end of the room. The wide cooking area, set back into the wall and tiled on three sides for easy maintenance, adds to the horizontal look.

Cabinets and counters, both finished in laminate for a uniform look, are differentiated by a very subtle shift in color—from pale-gray to pale mauve. Stainless steel on the oven, refrigerator/freezer, and range (above)

harmonizes with the neutral colors. Flanking the set-in refrigerator are large pantry units designed for maximum storage, and directly opposite the sink/dishwasher area more cabinets allow convenient loading and unloading.

Along the sink wall and to the left of the built-in oven is a telephone counter created under another window (right). Here, adjustable shelves are built into the small space against the end wall to provide open storage for radio, speakers, and accessories. The counter provides a place for plants, notes, messages, and household planning, and the drawer below can hold all the pencils, pads, and other materials that tend to accumulate on most kitchen counters.

Bold color characterizes this contemporary kitchen, providing a handsome backdrop for the family as well as cooking students. Cabinets are faced with dramatic cobalt-blue laminate and finished inside in gleaming white. Counters and backsplash areas are sparkling white laminate to bounce light off work surfaces. Four main work areas divide the large, high-ceilinged room. In the center is a long island (left) with a drop-in electric range. The butcher-block top provides a place for food preparation, and around two sides is an overhang so friends or students can watch the action. Stools snug away under the ledge. The hood, faced to match cabinets, drops from the ceiling. Beyond the end of the island is a small sink beneath a clerestory that replaces parts of four windows, sacrificed to gain storage. And built into a counter behind the island is a hot tray. Fully accessorized interior cabinet spaces (left, bottom) include stepped-back spice shelves, swing-out wire baskets for oils and vinegars, and wine storage cells near the floor. A second cooking area (below), with two gas modules set into a peninsula and slide-out wire baskets for additional cooking equipment, overlooks a breakfast/garden room with wicker furniture and a greenhouse window. For another view of this kitchen, see page 36.

Clean, white cabinets and appliances keep a compact, one-wall work area from feeling cramped, and a new island separates kitchen activities from an eating area while maintaining the room's openness. From the kitchen side (below) there are no hanging upper cabinets to block the light or view through the French doors that lead to the patio and garden outside. A butcher-block top makes the island's surface useful for all kinds of kitchen tasks, yet suitable for setting up as a buffet. Old-fashioned drawer handles fit in with original window moldings, and open shelving below provides additional storage for large serving dishes. Over the cooking surface a simple marble shelf is hung to hold everyday spices within easy reach. A heavy, white porcelain-on-cast-iron sink offers one basin for food preparation and a second for dish cleanup. From the dining side (right) the line of sight across the island is unobstructed. Cabinet fronts are broken only by four evenly spaced knobs at eye level, just above the hood's control panel. The woods of the Parson's table, island counter top, and dishwasher chopping-block top all blend with each other and with the warm mustard-color wall. The darker cinnamon color, which visually lowers the ceiling of this 100-year-old home, picks up the tone of the parquet floor. Both walls and ceiling colors are repeated in some of the accessories displayed on open shelves over the refrigerator. The contrast between the dark, warm colors and white cabinets and appliances creates a lively and inviting feeling that maintains the home's original character.

Within a small, high-ceilinged space in an older home, this well-planned kitchen offers plenty of storage, both closed and open, and lots of light for working. Paneled cabinets give the room a somewhat formal look and blend with the old-style window trim. They run nearly all the way to the ceiling (above) for enclosed storage above the ovens, over the refrigerator, and in a corner. Warm, medium wood tones contrast with white counters and are repeated in the hood's edging. Work areas use every inch of space and are tucked into recesses and corners. Over the gas cooktop a narrow shelf (right, below) provides a place to display animal platters against the accented tile wall, and other shelf strips (top, right) hold spices and condiments.

Drawer storage is used effectively for pots below the stove (top, center) and for utensils near the sink. The small corner between the newly installed windows (top, left) shows off the family "beasties" on curved, glass shelves set onto wood strips.

A sophisticated cooking center (right) dominates this elegant kitchen in an urban home. Its wide, tiled wall with an accent strip of darker tiles draws the eye, and the glossiness of the tiles is repeated in the marble landings on either side of the commercial gas range and in the mobile island's marble top. The shelf over the range is protected from heat by a steel skin below it. (This idea and design are similar to the one shown on pages 20 and 21, demonstrating how an idea can be used to good advantage in more than one kitchen.) Plenty of daylight enters the room through the skylight in the center, the large glass panes in the exterior door, and the high window over the sink counter. At night canisters in the skywell light the room, and additional lights behind the cornice over the range light the cooking surface.

Cabinets in a very light wood, with no hardware or paneling (left, top), add to the clean-lined look. A simple molding strip runs along their top edge, tying the line in with the molding above the cooking area and around the doorway. Marble counter tops and stainless steel fronts on the compactor and dishwasher continue the sophisticated feeling.

For all its sophistication, however, this is a real working kitchen with storage placed wherever possible. A top drawer to the right of the range (left, bottom) displays spices on wedge-shape blocks for easy retrieval, and immediately below them are heavy pots placed on convenient pull-out trays lined with rubber mats. The movable work island holds cutting boards in vertical slots and moves to whatever area needs additional space during food preparation. It can also function as an elegant serving cart for the dining room, seen just beyond the pass-through.

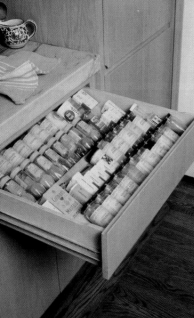

Blending old and new gives this kitchen excitement and sparkle. Traditional moldings around the six windows (left) provide old-style charm. However, a striking, stainless hood tube shoots down over the cooktop set against the window wall. A strip of brass edges the counters, and a surprising streak of pink neon light runs along the ceiling. Equally dramatic are the contemporary chrome theater lights hanging from the ceiling to light work areas. The stainless cooktop, which increases the cooking surface, is placed over a wall oven, set lower than usual. Stainless outlet plates, set horizontally, carry out the chrome color theme, and floor boards echo the brass color. On the sink wall (above) old-style glass-fronted cabinets reflect the light and display dishes and stemware to add sparkle. The clean whiteness of the painted walls, tiled counters, and laminated cabinets makes the room airy, light, and crisp. A stainless sink, recessed below tiles, continues the room's basic design themes, as do the high-arched chrome spout and streamlined faucets. Note the jog created in what was once a shallow counter top.

Open to the adjacent family room (see page 4), this work space is uncluttered and extends the family's sense of style into the kitchen. The harmonious blend of woods—on cabinets, floor, counters, and hood—is unbroken even at the baseboards and toe-kick space. This approach is an excellent example of a monochromatic color scheme, discussed on pages 48–49. Flat drawer fronts, subtle door paneling, brass knobs, and a handsome crown molding at the high ceiling contribute to the quiet elegance of the design. Daylight comes from all sides, and streams of sunlight on the wood floor add yet another warm touch to the room's comfortable feeling. Work areas are well separated with a tiled cook wall on one side, a butcher-block preparation counter by the main sink, and a short, tiled counter by a smaller sink for drinks (left). At the stove area (right) stacked ovens leave room for pot storage on pull-out trays. Rough-hewn tiles lend an informal touch to the counters and backsplash, and the wood color is also repeated in the grout lines and cookware.

Rich, wood color and small-patterned wallpaper lend a cozy look to an open kitchen/dining area (left). The cabinet style, fabric shades, antique furniture, white-painted beams against the board ceiling, and domesticated animals on the tiles behind the cooktop all lend a distinctive country feeling to this inviting kitchen. Built into the open room is plenty of storage and work space. Drawers to either side of the cooktop hold utensils, and ample work surfaces make cooking easy and efficient. Next to the built-in ovens is a secondary cooking area—a small grill—for preparing quick meals or dividing cooking tasks. The center island faces family activities and provides even more work space. The double sink is set into one corner with the dishwasher immediately to its left. Behind the sink is a ledge for pulling up a couple of high stools.

From the island (right, bottom) dishes can be carried to the eating area, which is enlivened by yet another barnyard scene. A graceful hutch displays glass doors, and twin hanging lanterns match the wood color.

Additional storage is recessed into a wall (top, left). Here, wide drawers provide a home for linens, and open shelves hold cookbooks and a microwave. Unusual glass-fronted drawers (top, right) provide a rotating display of grains and a touch of color. Throughout the room the same dark blue is used in wallpaper, window fabric, and seat cushions, and a small red/brown dot is picked up in the cherry cabinets, counter edges, hood trim, and windowsills. With white accents this color combination represents one approach to the major/minor color scheme discussed on pages 48–50. For other views of this kitchen, see page 76.

DESIGNING YOUR NEW KITCHEN

The illustrated guidelines in this chapter
show you how to develop a new floor plan
and how to tie your design together.
The Shopping Guide helps you
select new products and materials, and
down-to-earth information on costs, schedules,
and contracts helps you complete your plans.

After looking at other kitchens and establishing what style you'd like in your own, you'll want to get down to the details of design. First you should take a close look at your Existing Plan. It may be a square, rectangle, corridor, or some other odd shape. It may abut other spaces, portions of which could be annexed, or it may be that these spaces are already too small for their purposes. You'll want to decide how much total space you are willing to consider coopting to create your new kitchen.

You may find that during the initial stages of design, it is difficult to see your kitchen in new ways. However, you want to avoid approaching your design in a timid and hesitant way, making only slight modifications on what already exists. To counteract this tendency, spend some time creating layouts that include anything and everything you would like in your ideal kitchen, regardless of cost. If you're on a limited budget, this may sound like a waste of time, but it really isn't. Not only is this exercise fun, but it also fires your imagination, and imaginative ideas are particularly important when you're on a budget. Further, you should be aware of a few facts about your plumbing and wiring, which can sometimes be crucial factors in the design and construction of a new kitchen.

Plumbing. You can completely update and refurbish your kitchen without relocating a single wire or pipe, but if you want to rearrange the whole room, you may have to tear into walls and floors to get at these systems.

Efficient work and storage areas have been designed for a kitchen that must accommodate both a family and cooking students. Here, a central island with an overhanging block top allows people to pull up to the focus of activity. Behind the cook, a sink, built-in ovens, and refrigerator/freezer are within a few steps. Thus, the basic floor plan puts a compact kitchen core within a larger layout (see pages 22–23).

Nevertheless, you should know that you can move your sink a few inches to the right or left of its present position by stretching the flexible supply lines. Using your present supply lines, you can also add a second sink—for salad making or bar use—with its own shutoff valve. If you want to move the sink more than a few inches, you will need to extend the supply and drain lines, maintaining the code-required slope to the waste stack. If you have a bathroom above the kitchen or behind a wall, you may be able to tap into its supply and drain lines. In most situations you can move plumbing fixtures up to 6 feet from the existing vent lines without having to install all new plumbing lines, and the expense of relocating or installing new ones may be more dependent on whether or not you have easy access to these lines than on the distance you move the fixtures and appliances.

Gas and Wiring. You can also move a gas appliance a few feet to the left or right by lengthening the flexible tube from the gas valve. However, this valve must remain easy to reach in case of emergency, and local codes may specify the maximum distance you can move an appliance away from it. Electrical appliances can be moved anywhere as long as you have the necessary wiring in the new spot. The only limiting factor might be the placement of the hood and vent system over the proposed range or cooktop location. If you can run the ducts across a wall and out, directly out, or down and out, you have many options. If you have to run them upward through a second floor, you will need more extensive work.

Heating and Cooling. Moving your heating and cooling units may be simple, depending on the system. A radiator or baseboard heater can be relocated easily and the connections changed from beneath the kitchen floor. Forced air can be redirected by adding a new duct within a stud wall. Individual heaters can be added anywhere you have the electrical capacity.

If you are uncertain about some changes because of cost, try to create some options for yourself. You can usually make an educated guess about which of any possible alterations cost the most. Try to come up with at least two alternative plans: one that includes all the changes you want and another less expensive or less complicated choice. If you just don't know, go ahead with your plans, placing fixtures and appliances where you want them, and then check with a professional about costs.

Ordering Your Ideas

As you start tapping into your creative abilities, you may be flooded with so many ideas that it is difficult to settle them down into some sort of order. However, despite the fact that designing is not a straight, step-by-step process, it does have inherent logic. Kitchen design is best approached by focusing on the activities that occur in this room, deciding where you would like each of them to take place, and how you would like them to relate to each other. Then you can plan the specific appliances, counters, and storage spaces you'll need for each and tie them together into a functional layout.

When you're satisfied with a layout, you can draw elevation sketches of each wall and carefully plot out the types of cabinets, drawers, and shelves that you will need to create the efficiency you want. Only when

you've established the location and function of your storage units should you focus on the finish treatments that will tie your design together. The balance of this chapter is organized around these procedures.

Sample Plans

On the next three pages you will find floor plans of three different types of kitchens. For each kitchen there are three plans—the Existing Plan and two alternatives. One alternate entails relatively minor structural changes and the other more substantial ones. Note that no matter what shape or size your kitchen is, or how major or minor the remodeling, you can affect dramatic changes. Start your design process by using these sample plans to see what can be done in any kitchen space and to help you see the possibilities for your own kitchen. Then move on to develop your own layouts, following the guidelines in the remainder of the chapter.

When you begin sketching your plans, try including new elements like a clerestory over cabinets, a greenhouse window, open shelves, or a skylight as shown in the kitchen below (and on page 7).

SAMPLE PLAN 1

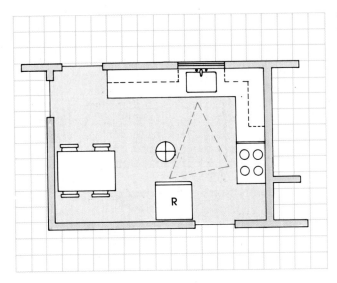

Existing Plan

The major problems in this rectangular kitchen include limited and inconvenient work areas and storage space, inadequate lighting, major traffic jams at the northeast corner, and an eating area that feels disconnected from the rest of the room. Plan A entails very few structural changes and yet the entire kitchen is altered by creating efficient storage and work spaces. Plan B requires relatively simple structural alterations to completely change the room's traffic pattern and to create a much larger work area. Both plans include new lighting and changes in the eating area. As new layouts are planned, ideas for new finish treatments emerge as well, and a new, cheery kitchen begins to take shape.

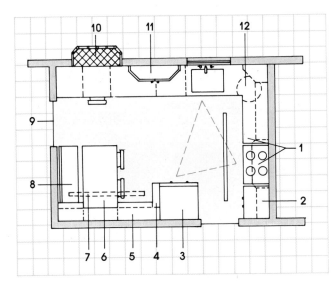

Plan A: Minor Structural Changes

1. Vent and fan added above range; roll-out shelves to left.

2. New upper and lower cabinets to right of range.

3. New side-by-side refrigerator/freezer; storage above.

4. Floor-to-ceiling, 12-inch open shelves.

5. Open shelves above wide, lower drawers for linens.

6. Table folds up to enclose open, upper shelves.

7. Track spot lights vastly improve the room's lighting.

8. Upholstered bench with lift-up top for storage.

9. Doorway to dining room is moved to make room for counter.

10. Outside door is replaced by a greenhouse window and desk.

11. New glass-fronted upper cabinet.

12. Turnaround shelf in base cabinet.

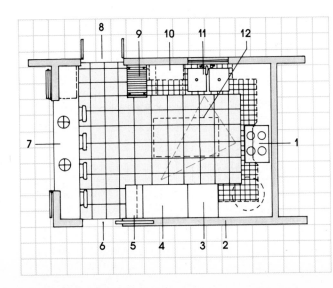

Plan B: Moderate Structural Changes

1. Cooktop centered in all-new cabinet wall.

2. Entry from hall closed off; new corner units installed.

3. Install wall oven and microwave.

4. Add freezer with enclosed cabinet above.

5. Built-in bar with shallow shelves for glass above.

6. Create new pocket doorway from living room.

7. Install buffet counter, close off doorway from dining room, and open wall for pass-through.

8. Replace old door with French doors to patio and garden.

9. Movable chopping cart with knife storage and shelves.

10. Open, upper shelving; tiled counter over dishwasher.

11. New, extra-large sink.

12. New lighting recessed under diffuser panel.

SAMPLE PLAN 2

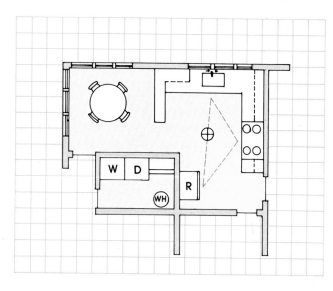

Existing Plan

The shape of a kitchen may be determined by its surrounding spaces. In this case the utility room creates some cumbersome problems. The refrigerator is isolated against the utility room's end wall and the side wall is virtually useless. Although the eating area has good, natural light, the table floats in the space and the whole kitchen lacks a sense of unity and integration. Plan A annexes part of the space from the utility room, softening the kitchen's sharp lines, and includes a window seat by the corner windows. Plan B entails stripping the kitchen and utility rooms bare and completely reversing the areas in which major activities occur.

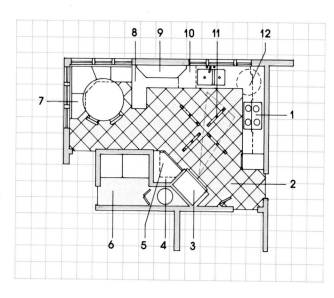

Plan A: Minor Structural Changes

1. New stove with fan, vent, and light; drawers below.
2. New floor tiles laid on the diagonal.
3. Utility wall rebuilt to house new refrigerator; cabinet above, corner desk and broom closet added.
4. Built-in shelves above telephone/work desk.
5. Light soffit with recessed spots.
6. Washer and dryer in same location as before.
7. Corner window storage seat with cushioned seats and back.
8. Counter extended to provide more surface and storage.
9. New upper cabinets.
10. Dishwasher added.
11. Track lights to improve task lighting.
12. Turnaround shelf in corner of base cabinet.

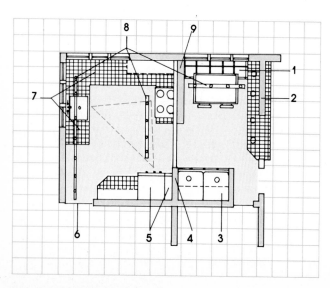

Plan B: Major Structural Alterations

1. Built-in upholstered bench in new eating area.
2. Pass-through tiled storage counter; recessed spot lights above.
3. Relocate washer and dryer and enclose with bi-fold doors.
4. Tear out utility room and install support beam.
5. Relocate hot water heater; install side-by-side refrigerator and narrow cabinet.
6. New doorway by refrigerator landing.
7. Move all work surfaces to old eating area.
8. New track lighting for working/eating; spots over serving.
9. Two-sided cabinet hangs from beam behind range.

SAMPLE PLAN 3

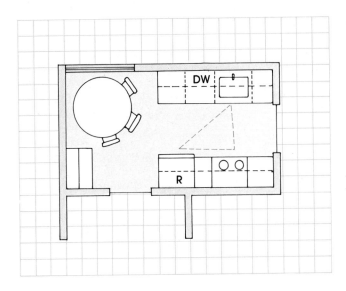

Existing Plan

This corridor kitchen is the one shown on page 13 in Chapter One. Even with a space as limited as this, the possibilities are extensive. Plan A requires no structural changes. Instead, attention is focused on restructuring all work surfaces and storage spaces to create an efficient space for two active cooks without sacrificing the eating area. Plan B includes moving one wall to recess the refrigerator. By running the counter all the way around the end wall, a substantial amount of additional storage space is gained. To develop a floor plan such as the ones shown here, you can follow some simple procedures, which are outlined on the following pages. Plan A is used as an example to illustrate this design process.

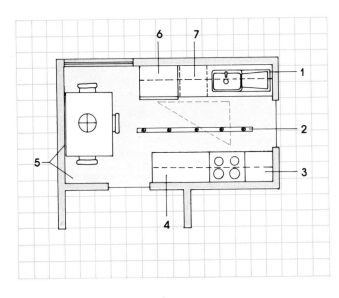

Plan A: No Structural Changes

1. Increase counter space to 18 inches wide—enough to accommodate a drainboard with deeper sink.
2. Install track lighting.
3. Widen counter to 24 inches and tile for pot landing.
4. Move refrigerator to create long baking center.
5. Remove old hutch and replace round table.
6. Remove unused counter and install refrigerator.
7. Install new upper cabinets all around kitchen and position hinges for convenience, particularly above dishwasher.

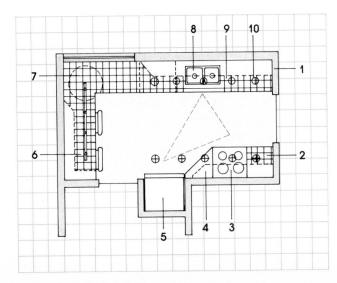

Plan B: Minor Structural Changes

1. Replace half-walls near dining room with full walls and add doors to create privacy.
2. Increase counter space to 24 inches and tile.
3. Install new freestanding range with self-cleaning oven below, microwave above.
4. Counter angled to create easier access to new, recessed refrigerator.
5. Double-door refrigerator/freezer recessed into pantry area to eliminate conflict with open dishwasher.
6. Table-height counter installed on end wall with track lights above.
7. Counter turns corner with ample storage cabinets below. Turnaround shelf in corner.
8. New, double sink replaces old, shallow one.
9. Counter width expanded for additional work space.
10. Recessed spots added to improve task lighting.

DEVELOPING A FLOOR PLAN

To develop your own floor plans, review your Kitchen Survey and your Priorities List. Then tape a sheet of tracing paper over your Existing Plan and sketch in the general outlines of your present kitchen space and any adjacent area you might consider using.

Activity Centers

You may want to begin by laying out your counter space in some basic shape such as a U or an L, but you'll develop a more workable plan if you let the shape of your layout evolve as you go along. The first step is to decide where in your kitchen you want to do what. Do you want to work near the window, or would you rather eat there? Would you like a major work center in the middle of the room? Think generally at the outset to retain a sense of the whole. Sketch circles or ovals to represent your various activity centers—eating, cooking, cleaning up, baking, menu planning, laundering, and so on—and play around with these circles to get a sense of the different ways you might use your kitchen space. Choose two or three alternatives that spark your imagination and excitement, and start sketching in more detail. Unless there is another more compelling area you want to start with, begin with your major work areas at the sink, range, and refrigerator.

Major Appliances

Cut out index cards or use a plastic template to draw in your major appliances. Move them around on the tracing, placing them where you'd really like to have them even if the whole room changes. If moving them from one side to the other doesn't work, consider using an island or peninsula. Keep starting fresh rather than fussing with one idea. Brainstorm. Experiment. Try just about anything, regardless of cost considerations, because you may hit on ways to save money even if you relocate pipes and wires. Look at the way doors and drawers will open—you won't want the open dishwasher door to block the refrigerator door, for example. If none of your alternatives work comfortably, you may need to scale down the appliance sizes you've chosen. Or consider moving windows, doors, or walls. Even minor structural changes might help you create a workable kitchen. The work triangle will change with each new arrangement of appliances, so trace a plan whenever you find one you like.

Minor Appliances

When you have one or two configurations you like, fit in your other appliances. Choose which side of the sink you'd like to place the dishwasher, leaving yourself at least 20 inches in which to stand. If you want a trash compactor, place it somewhere near the cleanup area. Decide whether you want a new microwave to be part of an oven wall or on the counter. Locate it where you would do your quick cooking. If you'd like a separate freezer, see how a horizontal or vertical unit would fit into your plan. Plot possible locations for your laundry appliances. If you want a TV, mark an X where you would like to place it.

---

1. Existing kitchen. Some of the problems to be solved in the same kitchen shown on pages 13–15 include: the conflicts between refrigerator, oven, and dishwasher doors; inconvenient and small work surfaces; the lack of drawer space; the crowded eating area, the lack of a well-defined baking center, and poor lighting.

2. Activity centers. Within the room's basic shell, rough circles show desired activity areas—cook and serve, prepare and clean up, eat and read. In this sketch, the locations are about the same as before, but several other sketches move the areas around the room, closing off doors and opening up walls. To save money, this one becomes the final choice.

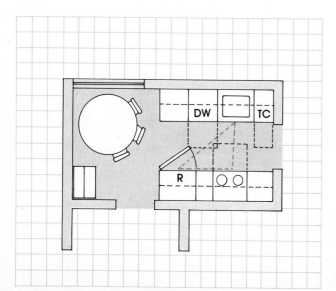

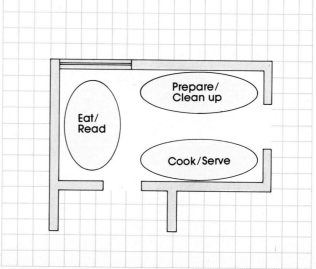

Work Surfaces

Block out work surfaces next, and work with the standard 2-foot, front-to-back counter depth. Decide what chores you will do to the left and right of the sink. You'll need at least 24 inches on one side for a dishwasher. Experts recommend 24 inches on both sides, and more if you have to use one counter in conjunction with two appliances. Plan the space to the left and right of the range or cooktop. Here, too, experts recommend 24 inches as the minimum, but 30 inches would be better if you will also use the area for slicing, serving, or making pastry. Try to place an 18-inch counter next to the open refrigerator door. If the refrigerator shares space with another appliance, 36 inches would be better. Wherever you have trouble creating enough work space, try angling one or more appliances across a corner to pick up additional space to either side. Also consider supplementary work surfaces such as pull-out cutting boards and movable chopping blocks.

Storage

Although you'll plot out most of your storage details on your elevations, adjusting work surfaces also affects storage units. For now, think about the types of things you'll store in each area. Bear in mind that standard modular cabinets increase in size by 3-inch increments, and adjust surface spaces accordingly. Wall cabinets are generally 12 inches deep, so if you want to indicate any upper storage units, sketch in a dashed line halfway back from the edge of the 24-inch counter. For corner work surfaces, consider diagonal corner cabinets. Because tall storage units are separate from work surfaces but take up additional floor space, include pantry units and broom closets in your plan at this point. Don't worry about connecting the work spaces with one another—focus only on planning space around each appliance.

Other Activity Centers

When your work areas are positioned, start integrating them with other activity centers. Focus on the most important activities first, and see how you can use some areas for several different activities.

Eating area. Plan an eating area in conjunction with your work triangle so it is not too close to the range, sink, or oven but is convenient for serving and is out of the traffic flow. You may need a counter for quick breakfasts or a large table for visiting with friends and family, paying the bills, or reading the Sunday paper. Try a window seat. You can set it into a deep window, bump out a new space, or create one with cabinets. On either a peninsula or island, try incorporating an eating counter—stepped up, stepped down, or at the same level. If space is at a premium, consider some sort of mobile table that can be tucked away under cabinets or a table that pulls out of a cabinet.

Hobby and entertainment areas. Any of the counters and tables above might also function as a sit-down area for sewing, crafts, or model making. A cabinet below might offer space for a swing-up shelf for a typewriter or sewing machine.

3. Appliances. The refrigerator is moved to see if a workable triangle is formed. Although the dishwasher door now opens freely, the refrigerator door opens across the dining room entrance, and there is no counter space between the sink and refrigerator. Other options are tried until one or more workable triangles evolve.

4. Work surfaces and other activity centers. The refrigerator is moved again, leaving space for counters on either side of the sink and creating ample work surfaces—including a baking center—on either side of the range. A window seat and storage unit tie the eating area to the rest of the room, but the large table looks cramped and out of proportion.

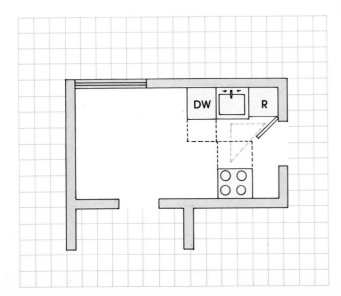

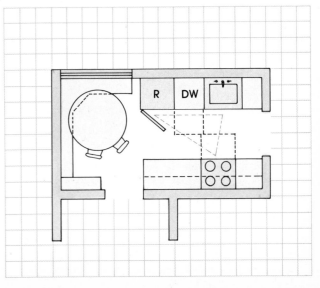

DEVELOPING A FLOOR PLAN

Traffic Patterns

Once you have planned all your primary activity centers, try tying them together in a way that creates an efficient and convenient traffic pattern. On a sheet of tracing paper over your work triangle and activity centers, rough out some possible traffic patterns. Draw arrows from your interior and exterior doors across the spaces between. How will people enter and leave the room? Where will they congregate? Where might several activities be going on at once? Begin establishing the traffic flow by connecting your various counter surfaces, using the recommended 4-foot aisle space. If traffic still flows through your work areas, try diverting it with a peninsula or an island. Most peninsulas are 2 feet wide, but they can be wider. Try islands of different shapes and sizes, and turn them in different directions to channel traffic away from work areas. If islands or peninsulas don't work, consider moving doors to create a more workable traffic flow. Even a few inches can make a big difference.

Lighting

No matter how well you have planned your activity centers, they will be difficult to use unless you provide adequate lighting. Look at your door and window placements and sizes. Consider enlarging a window, adding extra windows, installing a greenhouse window, a skylight, or light well. Or put in a new sliding or French door to the yard or terrace. Then plan for the times you use your kitchen after dark. Try to think in terms of general illumination—for the entire kitchen or over an eating area—and specific, or task, lighting for work areas. For general illumination you may prefer an overhead fixture, a hanging lamp, tubes behind diffusers on the ceiling, or wall sconces on either side of a table. For task lighting consider fluorescent tubes mounted under the wall cabinets, recessed spots, or track lighting. Several tubes will cast an even light over a whole counter area. Several spots or canisters can be directed to cast light on specific areas. A dimmer control will give you a wide range of light levels for different uses.

Draw Your Plan to Scale

When you've found a layout that feels comfortable, connects your various work surfaces, includes a smooth traffic pattern, and indicates lighting sources, draw the floor plan to exact scale. You may need to adjust here and there to get it all in as you have envisioned it so far, and you should fuss as much as you like until you're satisfied. Include all the details you've worked out.

Mechanical Systems

To complete your floor plan, note your plumbing, wiring, gas, and heating needs. Indicate where you'll need plumbing and electrical connections; plot light switches, outlets for small appliances, and decide whether or not you want to wire or plumb an island. Note new locations for gas lines and heating ducts. When all such notations are made on your plan, you can move on to elevation sketches to detail your storage units and then tie your design together.

---

5. Traffic patterns. The round table is replaced by a rectangular one that fits snugly to the built-in bench. However, the outer chairs obstruct the open refrigerator door and people trying to get into or out of the built-in seating area; it may be that the bench won't work. Traffic from the dining room is clear, and counter surfaces immediately inside mean that dishes can be put down or picked up with ease.

6. Lighting and scaled drawing. The built-in bench is removed to gain space, and the whole area seems more workable. A hanging light fixture is planned for the eating area, and a row of track spots beams light toward the four work areas. The dimensions of counter widths are finalized, the lines drawn to scale, outlets and switches indicated, and the plan is ready for elevations.

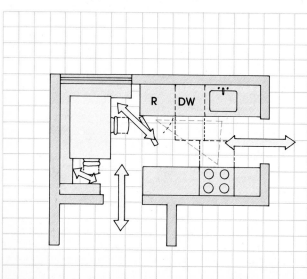

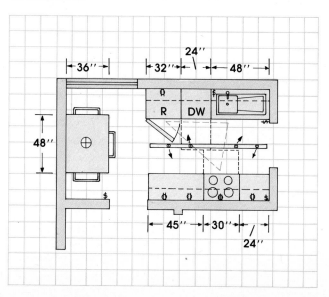

PLANNING STORAGE UNITS

Elevations

When you're satisfied with your floor plan, you should look at the walls head on. To do this, draw four elevations—one for each wall. If your plans include an island or peninsula, you may want to separate elevation sketches for these as well. On each sketch indicate the location and dimensions of all your kitchen elements, including doors, window openings, counter tops, and appliances. (Counter surfaces are usually 36 inches from the floor, and upper units begin 18 inches above that surface.) The main purpose of these first elevations is to detail your storage needs. You have probably already determined some of the basics on your floor plans, adjusting counter surfaces to accommodate standard cabinet widths, planning corner cabinets, and so on. Now you want to look at all these potential storage spaces in very specific detail.

Look closely at each work area, and list all the items you need to accomplish your tasks in that area. Draw circles in each area to represent a potential storage unit and list the items you'll want there. Then think through the activities that will take place in each work area. By the range you'll be getting out pots and pans, finding lids, reaching for spices, getting spoons and spatulas, or grabbing oven mitts or pot holders. Where do you want these items, and in what way do you want access to them? Do you want pots in a drawer, on a pull-out shelf, or hanging on hooks? Would it be easier to have spices on an open shelf on the wall, in a drawer, or on a turnaround shelf in a cabinet? Do you reach for them with your right or left hand? If you have expansive wall space designated for food, try different ways of dividing that space. Divide it according to food categories and to the way you use these food items. You may want a separate, lower shelf for the children's snack foods, for instance, or one for baking ingredients.

When you've allotted the space according to function and efficiency, get more specific about dimensions. Establish the cabinet widths you want and whether you want one or two doors. Check the chart on page 55 and your brochures for standard dimensions. As noted earlier, base and wall cabinets increase in width by 3-inch increments, and upper cabinets are generally placed 18 inches above the counter surface. They can go all the way to the ceiling or stop below it. You can leave the space above cabinets open or you can close it with a soffit. Figure out how high you want each shelf and how deep you want drawers. Include specialty items like turnaround shelves in corner cabinets, tip-out drawers in front of the sink, bins for potatoes, and so on.

Follow this procedure for each wall until you're satisfied that your storage units will meet your needs and are of appropriate dimensions. It's a good idea to take some time with this step. An extra few hours of finessing at this point could make the difference between storage units that are exactly what you want and those that aren't quite right. You may need to make some final adjustments on your floor plans, and sketch in the way you want doors to open so you don't inadvertently build in door and drawer conflicts.

General storage categories. Use circles to indicate what you want where. Plans for storage in this kitchen include: 1) casseroles and baking dishes; 2) cooking utensils; 3) pots and pans; 4) crackers, rice, and grains; 5) roasting pans and pot lids; 6) spices and baking ingredients; 7) knives, slicers, and graters; 8) baking equipment, placemats, and aprons; 9) cookbooks and telephone directories.

Specific storage plans. Previous ideas are altered and detailed to include: 1) teas, coffee, and mixes; 2) a swing-out spice rack; 3) cooking utensils, pots, pans, and lids; 4) cereal boxes; 5) broiler and roasting pans; 6) baking ingredients and grains; 7) baking dishes and utensils; 8) graters and small appliances; 9) knives, mats, aprons, and deep pans. Depths of shelves and drawers are carefully planned.

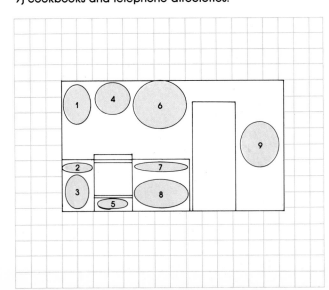

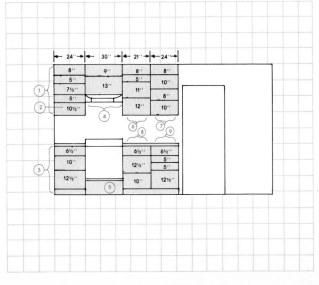

REFINING YOUR DESIGN

Refining a design—tying it together—is confusing to many people, but it needn't be. Like other stages of design, there are no hard and fast rules, but there are some basic guidelines. As you could see when you started sketching in storage units, your plan looks very different in elevation than in layout, and these sketches are very helpful at this point. Because cabinets and colors are so dominant in a kitchen, there's a tendency to choose these first and then make all other material selections. There's nothing wrong with this, but other important design elements can easily get lost along the way. Since most kitchens are inherently busy places, you want to achieve a state of balance in your design, and you can do this best with line, shape, pattern, texture, and contrast. These elements all work together to counterbalance any problems in your kitchen's shape and size, and give the room its overall tone. You can use your elevation sketches as tools for creating balance and harmony, and then choose a cabinet style and colors to support and highlight the foundation you've laid. Read through the simple guidelines outlined on the next few pages and look at the illustrations. Then look again at the photographs in Chapter Two with some of these principles in mind. You'll be able to see that this part of the design process does in fact have some logic to it.

Line. Place a sheet of tracing paper over one of your elevation sketches. Look at the vertical lines—doors, windows, refrigerator, wall ovens, range, pantry units, and cabinets above and below the appliances. They don't all have to be precisely aligned, but are there places where adding a few inches to the width of an upper cabinet would make it align with the edge of the sink or range? Look for places where vertical alignments would smooth out the lines in your kitchen without creating functional problems.

Look at the horizontal lines created by your floor, counter surfaces, upper cabinets, appliances, doors, and windows. Do they flow or do they jump all over the place? If they jump around and look a bit choppy, sketch some new lines. Even if you won't be able to reach high shelves, you may want to take the cabinets up to the ceiling simply because they look better that way. If you don't want your cabinets to extend to the ceiling, perhaps you can align them with the top of doors or windows. If you want shorter cabinets above the sink and range, make them both the same height. If you're thinking about installing a tile backsplash, consider the line created by the top row. Perhaps you can tie that line in with some other element in the kitchen or decide to run the tiles all the way up to the upper cabinet instead. When you're deciding where to install your wall oven, consider tying the top of it in with the base line of the upper cabinets or the bottom of it in with the counter-top line. Play around with your elevation sketches until the horizontal lines seem smooth and integrated.

When you're considering the type of cabinet style you want, bear in mind that the lines of these cabinet fronts create a visual effect. Horizontal slats on cabinet

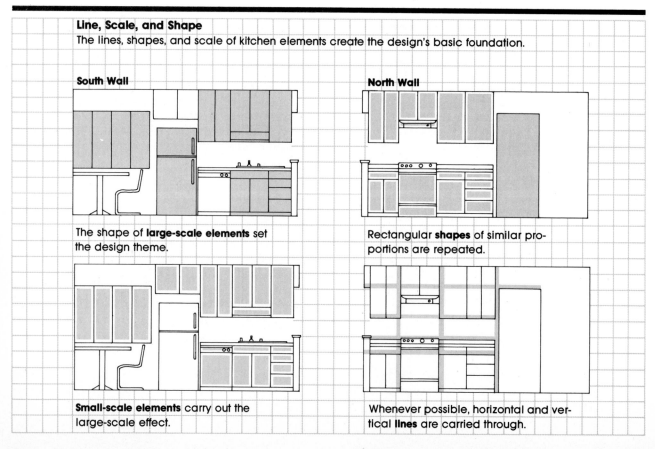

Line, Scale, and Shape
The lines, shapes, and scale of kitchen elements create the design's basic foundation.

South Wall

The shape of **large-scale elements** set the design theme.

North Wall

Rectangular **shapes** of similar proportions are repeated.

Small-scale elements carry out the large-scale effect.

Whenever possible, horizontal and vertical **lines** are carried through.

doors, for example, will elongate the kitchen, whereas vertical slats will draw the eye up.

Scale. Your kitchen has a certain scale, and the structural and individual elements within it will look best if they harmonize with that overall scale. If, for example, you have a very small kitchen, you may want to avoid expanses of closed cabinets or you may want to enlarge a window to increase the room's visual size. Look at the large-scale items in your kitchen—doors and windows, refrigerator, freezer, pass-through to another room, or an uninterrupted bank of cabinets. Are they in line with the overall size of the room or do they overpower the space? Then look at the small-scale elements. Do they harmonize with the large-scale elements? Are they of similar shapes?

Shape. Continuity in shape also lends harmony to your design, and you'll want to bear this in mind when you think about islands, peninsulas, windows, pass-throughs, tables, cabinet doors, and so on. This does not mean everything in your kitchen should be rectangular, for instance, but you'll want to avoid the jumbled effect created by a combination of too many shapes—large square windows, vertical upper cabinets, square base cabinets, arched doorways, carved soffit trim, a round table, and so on. Color in the various shapes you've created in your design to see whether or not they seem harmonious. If you've introduced an odd shape somewhere, you may want to repeat it elsewhere to tie the scheme together.

Contrast. Without thinking about color, try out some light/dark contrasts on your elevation sketches. Light walls with dark cabinetry create one effect and dark walls with light cabinetry create a completely different one. Dark, horizontal surfaces against light, vertical surfaces and vice versa create yet two more variations. By trying out different combinations on your sketches, you'll see the striking differences they make, and you may discover that you have definite preferences. You may even decide that you want very little contrast in your kitchen.

Pattern and texture. Patterns have a certain texture, and textures often create patterns of their own. Therefore, these two elements can be considered together. Pattern does not necessarily mean a floral or geometric print—it is any repeated shape and includes the overall lines in your kitchen as well as things as subtle as wood grain. The chaos of too many patterns in a room may seem very obvious, but even all-white tiles have a grid pattern, which should be considered when choosing other elements. If you have a very high ceiling in your kitchen, a vertical, striped wallpaper pattern will overemphasize that height whereas a small print or grid pattern may diffuse it. Glossy and matte surfaces are both smooth, but because one is bright and the other is soft, each affects the feeling of texture in your kitchen differently. Try sketching patterns on your floor plans and elevations. Look at the textures and finishes used in other kitchens you like. Look for combinations that carry out the feeling you want.

Contrast, Pattern, and Texture

Patterns, textures, and light and dark contrasts are used to support and highlight the design theme.

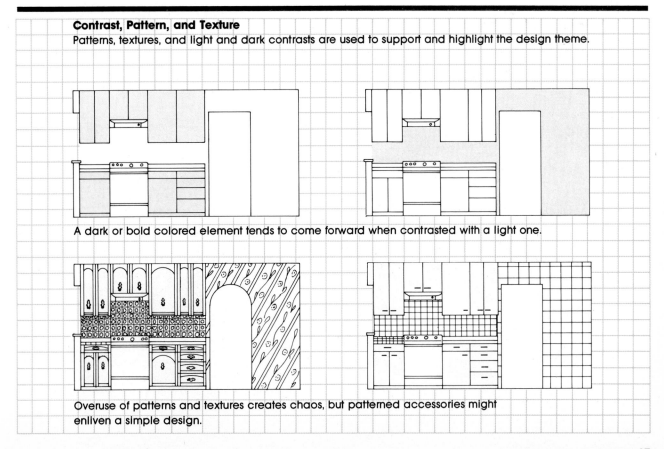

A dark or bold colored element tends to come forward when contrasted with a light one.

Overuse of patterns and textures creates chaos, but patterned accessories might enliven a simple design.

PLANNING A COLOR SCHEME

Choosing Color Families

How you select and apply color in your kitchen can make a big difference in your design. To select a color family (yellows, blues, greens, etc.), first take another look at the structural characteristics of your kitchen—its size, shape, and so on. Are there any features that you want to emphasize or minimize? Is there a dining nook you want to accent? Is the room relatively too long or too squat? Color can be used to compensate for architectural features you don't like and to accent those you do.

Dark and light colors. Applying the principles discussed in the section on "Contrast" (page 47), you can combine dark and light colors to achieve specific effects. For example, a dark color will visually lower a ceiling, whereas a light color will heighten it. Strips of color such as border tiles or wood trim used vertically will draw the eye up; horizontal strips will widen or lengthen the room. If you have some kitchen element you want to feature, you can use more intense colors to call it out; or you can minimize an area or element by using softer colors. Bear in mind that an intense color is not necessarily dark—bright yellow can be just as intense and used in the same way as cobalt blue, for example.

Warm and cool colors. Different color families have distinct characteristics. Colors in the blue family, or those with underlying blue tones, are cool. They tend to recede, pushing walls and surfaces outward and making

a room look larger. Colors in the red/yellow/orange families, or those with underlying red tones, are warmer and tend to advance, bringing surfaces forward and making a room appear smaller. If you have a tiny kitchen, you may want to use cooler, lighter colors unless you want to emphasize the compact nature of the room. In the same way, you can use warmer, darker colors to visually reduce the size of a large kitchen, or cool colors to expand its apparent size even further. The effect of colors in the middle ranges depends largely on how much blue or yellow they contain. Blues and greens with a lot of yellow can appear warm, and reds or yellows with a great deal of blue in them will seem cooler. Even whites, grays, browns, and blacks can appear either cool or warm depending on the amount of yellow or blue they contain.

Quality of light. After considering the structural effects you want to achieve with color, look at the quality of natural light in your kitchen. Where does this light come from? Is it cool northern or eastern light, or warm light from the south or west? Do you want to emphasize or de-emphasize the quality of that light? Cool colors in a room flooded with southern light may offset the heat of such light, whereas warm or bright colors may intensify it. If your kitchen receives northern light, cool colors can appear even cooler, and dull colors even duller. Warmer colors can be used to counterbalance this cool

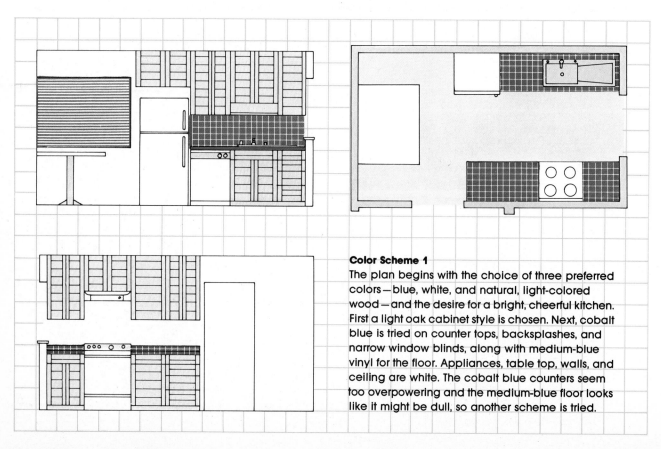

Color Scheme 1

The plan begins with the choice of three preferred colors—blue, white, and natural, light-colored wood—and the desire for a bright, cheerful kitchen. First a light oak cabinet style is chosen. Next, cobalt blue is tried on counter tops, backsplashes, and narrow window blinds, along with medium-blue vinyl for the floor. Appliances, table top, walls, and ceiling are white. The cobalt blue counters seem too overpowering and the medium-blue floor looks like it might be dull, so another scheme is tried.

natural light. You can also use the principles of contrast to create another kind of liveliness in an otherwise dull room.

Personal preferences. Another decision regarding color families can be made with a quick "yes" or "no" answer to a simple question: Do you want your kitchen to have the same colors used in adjacent rooms? If you do, you've already narrowed your choices down to a specific range; if this is not a priority, your choices may be wider. Further, when you were first considering the design and style of your kitchen, you probably defined a feeling you wanted your kitchen to have—warm and cozy, cool and sleek, or perhaps a blend of both. With the characteristics of warm and cool colors in mind, you can choose a color family that will enhance this desired effect. Even if none of these factors suggest an approach to color, you may have your heart set on a particular kitchen element—a special wallpaper, natural wood cabinets, or an antique cherry table—that you can use as a basis for a color approach.

Color Schemes

As a color direction suggests itself from the considerations outlined above, you'll want to develop an overall scheme. As a general guideline, you can approach your color scheme in one of two ways: Use one color family throughout the entire kitchen, or use one color family on major surfaces and another on minor surfaces and elements. In the first approach, you might choose to treat all areas in white or in shades of tan and light wood tones. The effect in both cases is essentially monochromatic, giving a feeling of peace and security or of sleek sophistication. In the second approach, you may choose to use blue on the surfaces you want to feature and white on background elements and surfaces. Or you may use wood tones as well as blue on major surfaces, supported by white on minor ones. The effect in these cases is generally rich, lively, and bright. Simply by looking at color schemes in other kitchens, you can get an idea of which approach appeals to you—monochromatic or major/minor.

Developing a color scheme. With a general approach in mind, begin to plan out your scheme. Start with something you want to feature. If it's the cabinets, start with those; if its the cozy eating nook, start there. Or if it's the wallpaper you love, start with that. Then play. Use your elevation sketches and floor plans to try different combinations. Use pastel chalks, crayons, colored pencils, inks, or felt pens to color in copies of your plans. Get paint chips from paint stores, and play with various combinations.

If you're using a monochromatic approach, try various tints and shades of your color family on horizontal surfaces—floors, counters, ceilings—and another on ver-

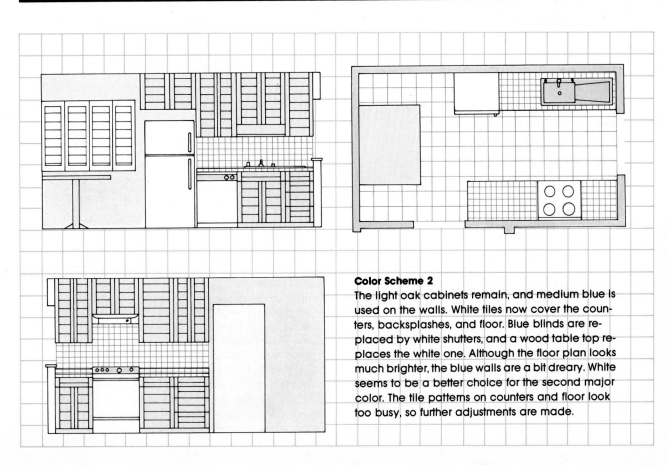

Color Scheme 2
The light oak cabinets remain, and medium blue is used on the walls. White tiles now cover the counters, backsplashes, and floor. Blue blinds are replaced by white shutters, and a wood table top replaces the white one. Although the floor plan looks much brighter, the blue walls are a bit dreary. White seems to be a better choice for the second major color. The tile patterns on counters and floor look too busy, so further adjustments are made.

COLOR, LIGHTING, & DETAILS

tical surfaces—walls, cabinets, appliances, and trim. Designers commonly choose the color for vertical surfaces first. Then they'll use that same color one tone lighter on ceilings and one tone darker on trim. If you're using a major/minor scheme, you may have a wallpaper or flooring pattern that has several colors in it. Pick out one of the colors; try it first on major surfaces and then on minor ones. Combine different tints or shades of each color on different surfaces to see which combinations you like best.

Because appliances are such a major item in a kitchen, their color can be crucial to your overall scheme. For the past two decades the basic appliance colors have been white, gold, avocado, and a copper brown, but this has begun to change: Commonly available colors now include almond and a chocolate brown, and finishes include black glass, stainless steel, and chrome. Try different colors on appliances. See how they look against cabinet colors. Perhaps you'll decide that white or almond would be easier on the eye than a colored appliance; or that a huge, black commercial range will completely dominate a wall that is already dark, whereas a commercial gas cooktop in stainless could lighten things up. Because sleek, black-fronted appliances create very bold accents in your kitchen, they should be used with discretion and only as an integral part of your color scheme. Some manufacturers provide kits for dishwashers and refrigerators that will hold insert panels, which match cabinet fronts. And finally, you can consider taking an old or new appliance to an auto-body paint shop for a custom color.

With all your various kitchen surfaces and elements, the idea is to keep playing with color combinations until you come up with a scheme that feels right. Look again at the photographs in this book and in your notebook. See how color has been used in these kitchens, and use these visual guidelines to aid your own choices. Then let your design goals, your chosen color scheme, and your own internal sense of harmony and balance guide your decisions.

Planning Your Lighting

When you were creating your floor plans, you considered the natural and artificial light that would increase your ability to work efficiently in your new kitchen. And as you worked with color, you analyzed the quality of the room's natural light. Now check for any areas that could use special attention. For example, you may have a corner for hobbies, eating, or household planning that deserves special lighting. You'll want to take a second look at these areas after planning their colors and patterns. Or you may have an area that receives strong sunlight, which can create hot spots on counters or tables, rendering them useless at certain times of the day. You'll want to plan window treatments that will minimize the effect of such strong light. Further, when natural light comes from only one source, it tends to create high con-

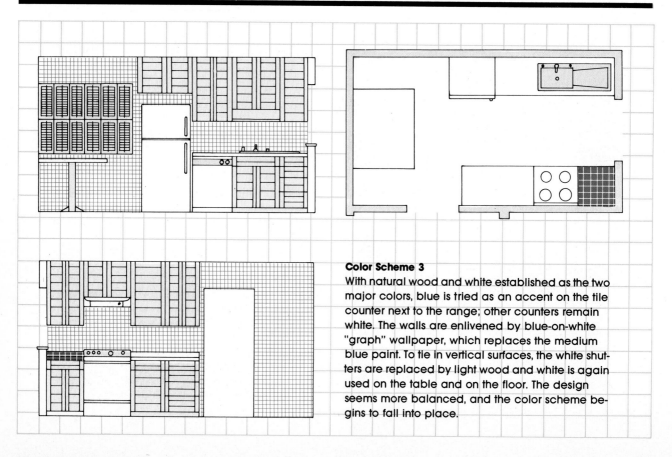

Color Scheme 3

With natural wood and white established as the two major colors, blue is tried as an accent on the tile counter next to the range; other counters remain white. The walls are enlivened by blue-on-white "graph" wallpaper, which replaces the medium blue paint. To tie in vertical surfaces, the white shutters are replaced by light wood and white is again used on the table and on the floor. The design seems more balanced, and the color scheme begins to fall into place.

trast between the window opening and surrounding walls, which can produce glare. Your kitchen will have more balanced natural light if it comes from two sources—through windows on two walls or through one window and a skylight. If this is impossible, you'll want to provide ample artificial lighting around your single source of natural light to soften the contrast.

You'll also want to make sure your artificial light sources are positioned so they will not create shadows over your work surfaces. Most kitchens used to have a single, centrally located ceiling fixture; however, standing between that light source and a counter or table blocks the light, creating a shadow. In your new lighting plan, you'll want to avoid this type of problem. If you want to use track lights, for example, position them so that light will come down directly over your work surface or, if the track is behind you when you're standing at a counter, position the light so that its beam comes down either from your right or left, not from behind you.

Fluorescent and incandescent lighting. Using incandescent or fluorescent lighting is a personal choice. Fluorescents are popular because they cost less to operate, give off less heat, spread light more evenly and generally, and are easy to install. On the other hand, incandescent light is warmer, truer, softer, and more flattering. Therefore, you may want to use incandescent lights for general illumination and over eating areas. Under-cabinet fluorescents will provide even task lighting on counters, but if you choose this type of light, be sure to select a bulb that comes closest to natural daylight.

Finally, look for balance in your natural and artificial lighting. Make sure that no matter what time of day or night you'll be using your kitchen, you'll have the lighting you want without harshness, glare, or contrast.

Details and Accessories

Before you consider your design complete, take a look at the room's detailing—molding, hinges, drawer and door pulls, hooks for oven mitts, holders for paper towels, and so on. The smallest details can complete your design or undo it. You can use something like a hand towel to create a single, bold color accent in an otherwise monochromatic color scheme. Horizontal door pulls can create yet another line that draws your eye back, which could be just right or the opposite of what you want. Narrow louvered blinds might be just the touch for your clean-lined kitchen or they could strike an odd note after you've worked hard to create the feeling of an old farm kitchen. Even exposed hinges could become prominent if the rest of your kitchen is highly streamlined—it might be better to use hidden ones. Look at all the details in your kitchen that will complete your design. Give them the same attention you've given everything else. Then, with your completed plans, you'll want to do some careful cost estimating.

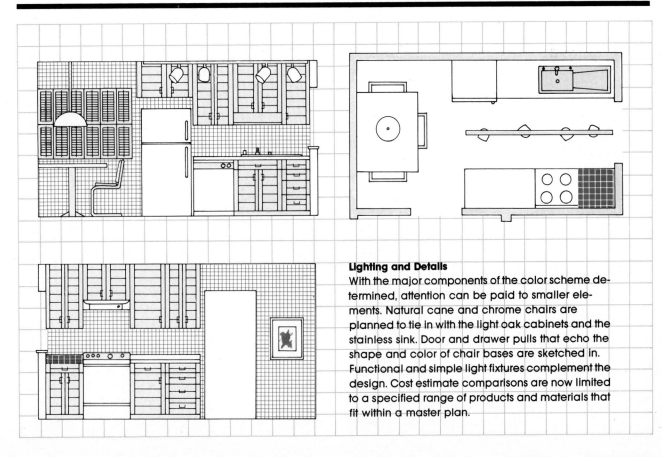

Lighting and Details

With the major components of the color scheme determined, attention can be paid to smaller elements. Natural cane and chrome chairs are planned to tie in with the light oak cabinets and the stainless sink. Door and drawer pulls that echo the shape and color of chair bases are sketched in. Functional and simple light fixtures complement the design. Cost estimate comparisons are now limited to a specified range of products and materials that fit within a master plan.

SHOPPING GUIDE

The charts on the following six pages are designed to help you make product and material selections for your kitchen. They are not exhaustive, and for every generality there is an exception. But because each selection entails choosing among several variables, you can simplify your shopping with some basic information.

Ranges, Ovens, and Cooktops

Your selection of cooking units will be vastly simplified by making a few initial decisions. First, decide whether you want gas or electric. Gas units heat and cool more quickly than electric ones and the flame is adjustable and visible, but gas ovens may have a tendency to dry out food a bit more than electric ovens, and the simmer heat setting on electric coils can be more stable. With most gas ranges you have a choice between a gas pilot light or electric ignition (which saves energy). Second, decide whether you prefer one or two ovens and a cooktop combined in a single range, or separate units. Third, determine which, if any, special cooking units might meet your needs, such as a microwave or commercial range. Fourth, decide whether you want freestanding, slide-in, or drop-in units. Most units come in stainless steel, enameled cast iron or steel, or glass fronted.

Cooktops

Type	Comments
Gas or electric	Set into a counter top much like a sink (see page 87 for installation instructions). Gas or electric connections are usually in the cabinet below. Venting can be through a hood above or through a downvent system below. Downvent cooktops may be more expensive but eliminate the need for a hood. Range in size from 3 to 6 inches high by 29 to 36 inches wide by 19 to 22 inches deep. Features: grills, griddles, plate warmers, rotisseries, reversible and interchangeable modules.
Smoothtop	Electric cooktops without visible coils; heated areas turn light yellow. Can take up to an hour to cool with no visible sign of lingering heat; turning the unit off requires special attention. Special pans and cleaning products prevent surface marring.
Magnetic induction units	Electric units that look like ceramic squares. Units may be placed anywhere and do not become hot to the touch as coils or smoothtop units do. Operate by magnetic transference of heat, requiring iron or steel cookware. Relatively high in cost.
Commercial gas	Made of heavy-duty cast iron with up to six burners in several styles. Usually 6 to 7 inches deep and with short legs for installing on a tile base. See example on page 27.

Wall Ovens

Type	Comments
Gas or electric	Operate by radiant heat. Gas or electricity heats the air, which heats the food. Single or double ovens available. Range in size from 31 inches high by 24 inches wide by 23 inches deep (single oven) to 50 inches high by 27 inches wide by 24 inches deep (double oven). Special features to look for: self- or continuous-cleaning, glass window in door, removable doors, clocks and timing devices. Decide on size and installation method before purchasing cabinetry.
Microwave	Operate with microwave energy, which causes water molecules in food to rotate at great speed, creating a friction that heats food very quickly. Foods don't dry out but browning can be a problem. Range in size from 13 to 16 inches high by 22 to 27 inches wide by 14 to 19 inches deep. Can sit on either a counter or shelf, be built into cabinetry, or purchased as part of a double-oven range. Features: button or dial settings, windows, temperature probes (oven turns off at designated temperature), timers, browning elements, turnarounds, rotisseries, and warranties.
Convection	Operate by heating and circulating air through the oven, reducing cooking time up to 33 percent. Good for browning, sealing juices, and cooking foods that need even heat (like roasts and cookies). Less effective for high-moisture-content foods that need to rise in the oven or be cooked in deep dishes (like cakes and casseroles). Most come with both radiant and convection options. Range from microwave size to regular range size. Relatively high in cost.

Ranges

Type	Comments
Residential	Come in both gas and electric, with one or two ovens, combining the features of cooktops and ovens. An electric range can have a coil, smoothtop, or magnetic-induction cooktop and/or a convection oven. A double-oven range can include a microwave or warming oven as the second unit. Come in freestanding, slide-in, or drop-in styles.
Commercial gas	Increasingly popular with active cooks. Made of heavy cast iron or stainless steel, have six burners but few of the special features of residential ranges. Relatively expensive. See pages 20 and 29 for examples of these ranges.

Hoods

Ducted vent hoods remove grease, smoke, heat, and moisture, venting them to the outside. Ductless hoods filter out smoke and grease but return heat and moisture to the kitchen. The Home Ventilating Institute rates the power of a fan or blower (blowers are quieter) in cubic feet per minute (CFM) and the loudness of the unit in sones. Better hoods have a minimum capacity of 300 CFM and loudness of less than 8 sones. Hoods are hung on the wall or ceiling 22 inches above the cooking surface. Vent openings are either round or rectangular.

Type	Sizes	Comments
Wall hung	6" to 30" high 21" to 24" wide (front to back) 24" to 48" long	Wall hoods can be installed under cabinets, under soffits, or against the ceiling. Facing materials are available in wood grains, stainless steel, copper, brass, and unfinished steel that can be built in behind wallboard or cabinetry. Enameled steel comes in many colors. Both types of steel are easy to clean. Copper and brass require special cleaning.
Ceiling hung	18" to 30" high 25" to 48" wide 36" to 120" long	Ceiling hoods can be attached directly to the ceiling or to a soffit. Come in the same materials and finishes as wall-hung hoods.

Refrigerators and Freezers

Size is your first consideration when selecting a refrigerator. An 8- to 10-cubic-foot refrigerator is generally enough for two people; add one cubic foot for each additional person. Three cubic feet of freezer space is adequate for two, and again, add another cubic foot for each additional person. Refrigerators usually stand out from 24-inch counters—only one company offers a standard 24-inch-deep "built-in" refrigerator, which is relatively high priced. You'll need to decide what type of unit you want—freezer above, freezer below, side by side, or under the counter (see below). Finishes are limited to enameled steel in a variety of colors and textured stainless steel. Some models have face frames in which you can insert a panel of your own choice, often a wood grain to match cabinetry. Consider the various features: seamless interior surfaces; number and adjustability of shelves in both cooling and freezing compartments, including the doors; location and range of temperature controls; self-defrost option; icemaker option; and energy efficiency factors (EEF's)—high ratings mean greater efficiency. Also, be sure the door swings in the direction you need or that it can be altered, and consider a separate freezer in either an upright or chest model for more storage.

Type	Freezer above	Freezer below	Side by side	Under counter	Upright freezer	Chest freezer
Height	63" to 66"	66" to 67"	65" to 68"	33" to 33½"	62" to 70"	34" to 37"
Width	28" to 33"	30" to 32"	33" to 48"	18⅝" to 19"	41" to 57"	41" to 57"
Depth	28" to 32"	29" to 30"	29" to 32"	19⅜" to 22"	25" to 32"	24" to 31"
Overall capacity	14 to 32 cu. ft.	18 to 19 cu. ft.	19 to 25 cu. ft.	4.1 to 4.3 cu. ft.	13 to 21 cu. ft.	9 to 18 cu. ft.
Cost	Moderate	Moderate	High	Low	High	Moderate

SHOPPING GUIDE

Sinks

Kitchen sinks are available with one, two, or three bowls in many different configurations. Sizes range from 12 to 48 inches long by 15 to 22 inches wide by 5 to 12 inches deep. Most sinks come with three or four predrilled holes for faucets, sprayers, or air gaps. Faucets are usually purchased separately. Special styles and designs are available. Sinks can be installed in one of three ways: recessed under the counter top, flush mounted with a metal rim, or hung by a built-in rim (called a self-rimming sink). See page 84 for methods of installation.

Sink Materials	Comments
Stainless steel	Probably the most popular material for a kitchen sink because it is very durable. Stainless steel is offered in either 18 or 20 gauge. The 18 gauge is heavier and sturdier. Steel that has a higher proportion of chrome in it requires less care and ages better.
Enameled cast iron	Heavy, durable, and available in colors. Quieter than enameled steel and less likely to chip. Easy to clean.
Enameled steel or porcelain on steel	Fairly easy to install and maintain. Lighter, noiser, and more likely to chip than cast iron. Come in colors.

Dishwashers

Dishwashers are either built-in or convertible. Their size has been standardized to 34 inches high by 24 inches wide by 24 inches deep. Finishes are much the same as those for refrigerators: enameled steel, brushed stainless, or special kits that allow you to select a finish of your choice, including wood grain. Portables often have a chopping-block top. Features vary from manufacturer to manufacturer, but look for: energy-saving features that allow high water temperatures for the dishwasher but low water-heater temperatures; cycles suited to your needs, such as rinse and hold, scrub cycles (which use very hot water to remove dried-on food), light wash, and no dry. Look carefully at rack configurations and styles to make sure they'll meet your particular needs.

Type	Comments
Built-in	Installed between base cabinet units. If placed at the end of a counter, an end panel can be installed to match cabinetry.
Convertible	Have special hoses and casters so they can be moved around. There are devices to convert this type to built-in. Some have chopping block tops for use as islands.

Garbage Disposals and Trash Compactors

Disposals are of two types—batch-feed and continuous-feed. Less expensive models have ⅓ horsepower motors; heavy-duty units have ½ to ¾ horsepower motors. Features: easy installation, sound insulation, and anti-jam mechanisms. Most compactors compress one standard grocery bag into a block or cylinder one-quarter of its original size. Several bags will weigh 20 to 25 pounds. Features: round or rectangular waste buckets, manual or automatic doors, drawers, or buckets. Finishes include black glass, brushed steel, and colored panels in an insert frame. Sizes are 15 to 18 inches wide, 18 to 24 inches deep, and 34 to 36 inches high.

Type	Comments
Batch-feed disposal	Activated when the cover is locked and turned to the "on" position and will not run when the cover is off. Easy to install but relatively expensive.
Continuous-feed disposal	Activated by a wall switch, and food may be added while the disposal is on, although this is not recommended. Expensive to install because it must be wired to the wall switch.
Compactors	Freestanding units on casters can be stored under or beside a counter. Built-in models are installed within the base cabinet line up and are front-loading.

Cabinets

The three main types of cabinets are stock, special-order, and custom. Stock cabinets are mass produced and come in standard modular units starting at 9 inches wide and increasing by 3-inch increments to 48 inches wide. Special-order units are offered by some manufacturers of stock cabinets. They vary in shape but come in standard sizes and generally have more accessory options. Delivery may take longer for these units. Custom units are made to your specifications by a local cabinetmaker who can ensure quality and design the units to suit your kitchen space. While style will certainly be one of your first concerns, quality is of crucial importance. Shop around and compare construction techniques. Also look for special features that aid efficient storage and easy access: adjustable, turnaround, and slide-out shelves; tip-out drawers for the dead space in front of the sink or cooktop; inserts for knife and spice storage; bins; and so on.

Cabinet Sizes

Type	Size	Comments
Wall hung	9″ to 48″ wide 12″ deep 12″ to 42″ high	Heights vary depending on whether or not the cabinet extends to the ceiling or a soffit, and whether it hangs over a counter, range or sink. Turnaround shelves for corner cabinets available.
Base	9″ to 48″ wide 24″ deep 34½″ to 96″ high	Available with doors, shelves, and drawers in various combinations. Drawers come in different depths. Tall units for pantry or broom closet and two-sided cabinets also are available.
Wall oven units	30″ wide 24″ deep 84″ high	Trim kits are used to fill gaps between ovens and cabinetry. Must know the size of the oven before ordering cabinet unit.

Cabinet Materials

Cabinet Part	Materials	Comments
Case parts (sides, bottom, and back)	Particleboard Plywood Hardboard (backs)	These three materials are the ones most commonly used for interior case parts. Particleboard is generally used as a filler between wood veneers and should be treated with a sealant to prevent it from absorbing moisture, which can cause swelling. Plywood is stronger than particleboard, more expensive, and gives the appearance of higher quality.
Face frames	Solid lumber	Quality cabinets always have solid-lumber face frames.
Drawer sides and backs	Plywood Solid lumber Particleboard Particleboard with a vinyl wrap	Plywood or solid-lumber drawer sides generally denote quality as long as all joints are sturdy and secure. Although particleboard can be used, it can fracture or crumble under heavy impact.
Face materials	Wood	"Solid wood" cabinets generally mean that both lumber and high-quality plywood have been used to construct face materials. In some instances the frame and fronts may be made of solid lumber.
	Plastic laminate	Plastic laminate comes in many colors and is easy to clean. The material should be solidly affixed to its base, which is commonly made of particleboard. Edges should be laminated or they can fracture and crumble. Usually less expensive than solid wood.
	Particleboard veneered with vinyl or wood	Used for door and drawer fronts. Edges should also be veneered or they can fracture and crumble. Inexpensive.

SHOPPING GUIDE

Cabinet Construction Techniques

Cabinet Part		Look for ...
Joints	Case parts (sides, bottom and back)	... screws, nails, and glue. Solid, sturdy feeling at all case joints. Backs should be firmly stapled.
	Paneled doors and face frames	... doweled, mortise and tenon, tongue-and-groove, or other interlocking joints, although some are constructed with glue and screws. Joints should feel solid and secure.
	Drawers	... joints that are dovetailed or made of some other interlocking construction. However, glue and nails are the most common—these should feel solid and secure.
Door and drawer fronts		... solid material or at least a substantial feeling throughout, and finished edges. Make sure drawer face is securely joined to the sides (see comments on drawer joints above).
Drawer slides		... sturdy slides solidly attached to cabinet with screws. Metal slides are the most common, but some wooden ones work well. Two side slides are generally better than a single, center one. Drawers should slide easily.
Hinges		... solidly attached hinges that feel secure. Some hinges are self-closing.
Catches		... ease in opening and closing doors. You shouldn't have to yank the door to get it open.

Surface Materials

Selection of counter-top, wall, and flooring materials is directed primarily by function, design, and budget. Durability is essential on counter tops and floors, and walls around the sink and range should be easy to clean. If you do a lot of cooking, chopping blocks or smooth baking surfaces may be important to you. As you develop your design, certain colors, patterns, and textures will begin to suggest themselves, and you'll want to go out and see for yourself what is available. Some basic characteristics of common surface materials are outlined below.

Counter-Top Materials

Type	Comments
Plastic laminate	Pre-laminated counter tops are available with or without edging and backsplashes or they can be custom ordered through your dealer. Laminate is easy to maintain, comes in many colors, patterns, and textures. Thicker plastic denotes quality. Subject to scorch and cut marks, which can be repaired only by patching. Will last 7 to 10 years under normal use.
Ceramic tiles	Glazed tiles are impervious to water, grease, and stains; unglazed tiles are not and are not recommended for kitchen counters. Can be tedious to install, but are extremely durable, easy to maintain, and provide the widest range of counter-top colors and patterns. Available sizes include 1- to 6-inch squares as well as mosaic tiles on a backing. Some mosaics are pre-grouted. Colored grouts available. All grouts should be sealed to prevent mildew and soil buildup.
Synthetic marble	Marble "look-alikes" include cultured marble—marble chips in a plastic resin—synthetic marble—made with methacrylate. Cultured marble is used more in bathrooms. Synthetic marble, known as Corian®, is becoming increasingly popular. It is durable and resistant to moisture, stains, cracks, and heat. Scratches can be repaired by sanding. Comes in slabs, which can be worked like wood with carbide-tipped power tools. Can also be used on walls. Expensive.
Marble	Used primarily for making pastries and candy because of its cool, smooth surface. Very heavy, scratches easily, can crack, but doesn't burn. Must be waxed and polished. Expensive.
Butcher block and wood	"Genuine" butcher block is made of thick, laminated pieces of hardwood end grain that are either untreated or oiled. Generally used on only a portion of a counter top or as a separate chopping block. The porous surface is easily marred and stained, although burn and scratch marks can be sanded away. Sealed with polyurethane, the surface is more durable but is no longer considered true butcher block. Wood counter tops with a polyurethane finish can be used for all counter-top surfaces. Will scratch and burn but are easily repaired. Relatively inexpensive.

Wall Coverings

Type	Comments
Paint	Latex enamel paint is easy to apply and maintain. Available in a vast range of colors, is relatively low in cost, and will last 3 to 10 years.
Wallpaper	Pre-pasted vinyl-coated papers are the easiest to install and maintain. Uncoated papers should be treated with silicone so they can be wiped clean. Installation is more difficult if you do your own pasting. Quality paper, properly hung, can last 10 to 20 years. Moderate in cost.
Wood paneling	Sheets of paneling, 4 by 8 feet, are easy to install directly to studs or wallboard. Easy to maintain if you avoid light-colored panels with rough textures that collect dirt and grime. Less expensive panels are usually made with a hardboard base and a simulated wood-grain veneer. More expensive ones have solid wood veneers and have the look and feel of quality. Installation instructions provided by the manufacturer.
Ceramic tiles	Tedious to install but will last a lifetime. Commonly used on backsplashes and around the range. Available in a wide range of colors, patterns, and textures, and standard sizes range from 2- to 6-inch squares. Mosaic and rectangular tiles also available as are colored grouts. Grout sealer necessary to prevent mildew and wear.

Flooring Materials

Type	Comments
Tongue-and-groove wood	Increasingly popular in kitchens, wood is long-lasting, strong, and looks very warm. Treated with polyurethane, it is impervious to liquids. Can be hard on the feet. May require extra care. Installation can be expensive and is best left to a professional.
Wood parquet tiles	Genuine parquet flooring consists of strips of wood laid in patterns. Expensive and difficult to install properly, it is best left to a professional. However, cushioned parquet tiles are available in 6- to 12-inch squares. They are easy to install and come in a range of wood tones and patterns. Wood quality varies and price is moderate to high.
Ceramic tiles	Extremely durable and available in a range of colors, shapes, and sizes; glazed tiles are impervious to water but are slippery. Unglazed tiles are less slippery but are porous, absorb water, and stain (except porcelain, which is very dense and therefore not porous). Cold to the touch and can be hard on your feet. Do not absorb noise. Moderate in cost.
Quarry tiles	Thick, heavy, and can be glazed or unglazed. Come in earth tones and in a variety of sizes, and shapes. Cold to the touch and can be noisy. Moderate in cost.
Sheet vinyl	Still referred to as "linoleum." Very durable, easy to maintain, and available in a wide range of colors, patterns, and textures. Some have cushioned backing and/or no-wax finish. Come in 6-, 9-, and 12-foot rolls. More difficult to install than vinyl tiles, but less chance of water seepage. Can tear and dent if treated carelessly, but can last up to 15 years or more with proper maintenance. Low to moderate in cost.
Vinyl tiles	Easy to install and maintain, but if not installed properly can chip or lift, and water can seep beneath. Wide range of colors, textures, and patterns. Some have cushioned backs and/or no-wax finish. Come in 8- to 12-inch squares and sold by the square foot. Low to moderate in cost.
Carpeting	Adds a warm feeling to the kitchen, is easy on feet, absorbs noise, comes in many colors, and is easy to install. Can be difficult to clean and is not as durable as other materials. Made of nylon, olefin, or polypropylene with a waterproof backing (which differentiates it from "outdoor" carpeting). Nylon has the highest resistance to fading, staining, and abrasion. Available in self-stick tiles or rolls.
Cork tiles	Self-stick square tiles with a polyurethane finish. Come in a variety of colors and are easy on your feet. Easy to install but have the same drawbacks as vinyl tiles.

ESTIMATING COSTS

To figure out the costs for your entire project, you need to make a list of all the materials you want to purchase, all the tools and supplies you'll need, and any services you plan to use. It's easy to remember things like the shiny new refrigerator and to forget little items like finishing nails, wallpaper remover, sandpaper, and so forth. You will need to know, for example:

☐ how much rough lumber to order to reframe a door, wall, or window, or to strengthen floor joists.

☐ the amount of finish lumber necessary to build a window seat, edge a counter, or trim out doors and windows.

☐ the size of ceramic tiles you want to use and the area they will cover. (Add 10 percent for breakage—more if you have to do a lot of cutting.)

☐ the types and numbers of plumbing and wiring supplies you'll need.

☐ how many switch boxes or receptacles you need for your new lighting plan.

The best way to determine what you'll need is to list all the materials, tools, and supplies required to complete each task you intend to do. You can review each one in Chapters Four and Five, and then make up your list. Use the sample on the facing page as a guide.

When your list is complete, shop around to get the best prices. You may be able to order from a catalog or through your designer or contractor, or you may want to pick up certain items from local retailers. Prices will vary with quality, from dealer to dealer, and from retailer to retailer. Be sure to get prices for possible substitutions in addition to your first-choice items. If you have your heart set on hand-painted French tiles, for example, you may find the total price—including installation—too high for your budget. But you may be able to use the hand-painted tiles as a border or backsplash and substitute less expensive tiles for the rest of the counter. You may also decide to install the tiles yourself to lower the price.

Professional Services

Which professionals you turn to will depend on what aspects of the project you want to do yourself. You can work with an architect, an interior designer, a kitchen designer associated with a kitchen dealer, a contractor, subcontractors, or any combination of these.

Architect. If you're planning a major renovation, consult an architect at an early stage. There are several different ways of working with architects:

1. The architect will draw plans for your approval and supervise the ordering of materials and construction by contractors.

2. The architect will draw up a complete set of blueprints. You can use them yourself or hire a contractor to do the building from the complete specifications.

3. You can pay for a feasibility study and a basic drawing, and then take them to a contractor who will insert cabinetry dimensions, specify appliances, and handle the construction.

Interior designer. You can use an interior designer in much the same way you'd use the services of an architect. The designer may charge a flat fee for the de-

signs, an hourly fee for supervision, and mark up costs for ordering materials; or the flat fee may include both drawings and supervision of construction. You will have to clarify this. A designer can be invaluable in helping you locate and select certain materials, fixtures, finishings, and furnishings. The customary cost plus markup is often less than retail price, and designers have access to dealers that you cannot buy from directly.

Kitchen dealers and designers. Dealers who retail kitchen supplies usually have one or more kitchen designers working with them, either on a full- or part-time basis. While knowledgeable about cabinetry, surfaces, and materials, these professionals may not be quite as experienced in structural or finishing materials, fabrics, and overall design as architects or interior designers. However, many of them can provide good advice and innovative ideas for use of space. Design fees are often credited against the price of cabinets and appliances purchased through the dealer.

Contractor. You can work with a general contractor in several different ways:

1. The contractor can produce drawings from which the kitchen will be built by the contractor's own workers and subcontractors.

2. The contractor can work from a complete set of blueprints supplied by your architect or designer.

3. The contractor can enhance less detailed plans drawn by an architect, designer, or yourself.

4. The contractor can specify and order materials, set up schedules, and supervise installation by various workers.

5. The contractor can supervise your work, checking it over carefully on a daily basis if necessary, and supervise subcontractors handling jobs that you don't want to do yourself.

Although contractors do not usually have the design experience of architects or designers, they deal with the realities of space, plumbing, wiring, and structure on a daily basis. This practical background provides many solutions to some of the trickier parts of remodeling.

Subcontractors. Specialists in plumbing, wiring, cabinetry, masonry, tile, and so on are paid by the hour or day for the time they spend building or installing all or parts of a kitchen. They don't draw up plans, but they may offer advice. Most subcontractors can work without your constant supervision, but if you have specific ideas about how you want certain things done, be on hand when that portion of the work is underway.

Choosing a Professional

Once you have located various firms or individuals with whom you might like to work, do some checking up. Ask to see any photographs of past jobs, other sets of blueprints, or recently finished projects. Get the names of two or three former clients and call them to see how satisfied they are with the work that was done. Go to see the finished kitchens to determine whether you like the workmanship, the ideas, the materials, and the finish details. When you've decided which professionals are your most likely candidates, get at least three bids.

Soliciting Bids

First decide what you want to do yourself and what you want a professional to handle so you'll know what estimates you need. Then spell out the nature of the job as clearly as possible so that all bidders will provide answers to the same questions. Get bids from several different professionals so you can compare estimates. It may not be necessary to get several bids for small tasks, like putting in a single window, because the difference in cost might not be worth the bother. But for big jobs—plumbing, cabinetry—you should definitely get competitive bids. You may have to pay a consultation fee, although some professionals provide free estimates in the hope of securing the job. You can request bids in several different ways:

1. If you intend to purchase your own materials, request estimates on design or labor only.

2. If you want the professional to order and pick up materials, request estimates for design or labor and for materials. If you want to do some of the work yourself, specify which parts you plan to do, but request estimates on them anyway; you may change your mind later.

3. Request an estimate solely for supervising specific parts of the project.

No matter how you make your request, be sure to ask for a breakdown of the total estimate according to specific jobs. You should also ask for an estimate of how long it will take to do the work. Compare these time estimates as well as those for labor and materials. Look for major discrepancies between bids. A low bid may be missing a crucial item, and a high bid may include something it shouldn't.

The Final Planning Stage

After you have evaluated your bids, you may have to make some difficult decisions about your project. If the estimates are way beyond your budget, you'll have to scale down some of your favorite ideas. This isn't nearly as much fun as drawing up your original plans, but don't despair. There are always ways of compromising without destroying your concepts. Ask your designer or contractor for ideas—they deal with these situations daily. Look over the substitutions on your materials list and review your priorities list from your survey. Even with compromises, your new kitchen will still be a vast improvement over your current one.

Cost Estimate Worksheet

The best way to estimate your costs is to make a list of each dismantling and installation task you're planning to do. Then, for each task, list all the new materials and products that will become a visible part of your new kitchen—cabinets, hardware, sink, appliances, surface and finishing materials, and so on. Next, list the unseen supplies you'll need, such as lumber, insulation, pipe, and electrical wire. And finally, list the tools you'll have to buy to carry out your tasks. Unseen costs can quickly mount up, so be thorough. Use the partial list that follows as a guide for creating your own.

Task	Items needed	Have	Buy	Rent	Price/unit	No. units	Estimated total cost
Install tile floor	Glass cutter/scorer		X				
	Tile saw			X			
	Carbide-tipped bit			X			
	Sand		X				
	Mortar		X				
	Serrated trowels		X				
	Tile spacers		X				
	Grout mix		X				
	Threshold		X				
Install sink, disposal, and dishwasher	Faucets		X				
	Spray attachment		X				
	Drain fitting		X				
	5/8-inch CDX plywood		X				
	Sink caulking		X				
	Hose clamps	X	X				
	Putty		X				
	Washers/slip nuts	X	X				
	Air gap		X				
	Pipe fittings	X					

Etc.

DRAWING THE FINAL PLAN

When you've reassessed your costs, decide what changes you need to make on your plans, and make a final drawing that includes them. You will use this drawing for approval by the building department, so it should be entirely accurate. It doesn't need to be professionally drawn, however, since most building departments simply want to see your Existing Plan and have a clear plan of your proposed changes. On the other hand, if your project includes major structural, plumbing, and wiring changes, you may want to get some help. Include all measurements of walls, doors, and windows, and show surrounding rooms.

To obtain a plumbing permit, you should show the location of all plumbing fixtures. Some building departments may want to see more, but you should start with the locations. The field inspector will make sure code requirements are met during installation. Requirements for electrical permits vary, but you should show all light fixtures, switches, and outlets on your plan. Whenever something is not clear, make notations.

It is usually unnecessary to draw elevations to obtain permits, but you may want to do so for your own purposes. You can call out all the actual materials and products you've decided to use, which will help you make sure you order everything you need.

The Final Materials List

Your final materials list functions as an order form, so it will include information that you did not need when you were estimating costs. Some manufacturers will provide forms for ordering your products or materials. Others will not. In either case, you will want to keep your own records. The best method is to make up a ruled sheet that includes spaces for the name of the object or material, model number, color, finish, size, quantity, and price. Add any special characteristics needed to distinguish it in ordering. Whenever you know a delivery date, indicate this in pencil in a far-right column. From these dates you can begin to plan your schedule. Be sure to follow all the manufacturer's instructions and dimensions, and write them down in the proper order. Some read exactly opposite from what you might think. For example, cabinets are grouped by their front-to-back depths and by category (base, wall, etc.), not by width and height. Go over your list several times to make sure all your specifications are correct.

The drawings on these two pages represent final plans for the kitchen illustrated throughout this book. Wall elevations are drawn to indicate heights, materials, and colors. Compare the drawings to the final result, pictured on pages 94 and 95.

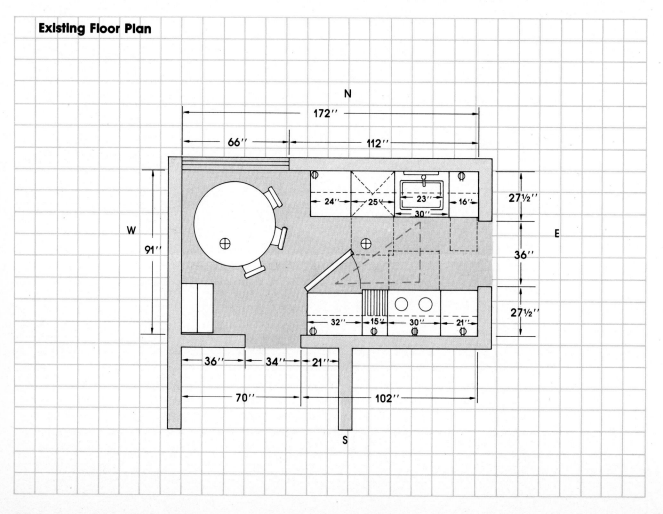

Existing Floor Plan

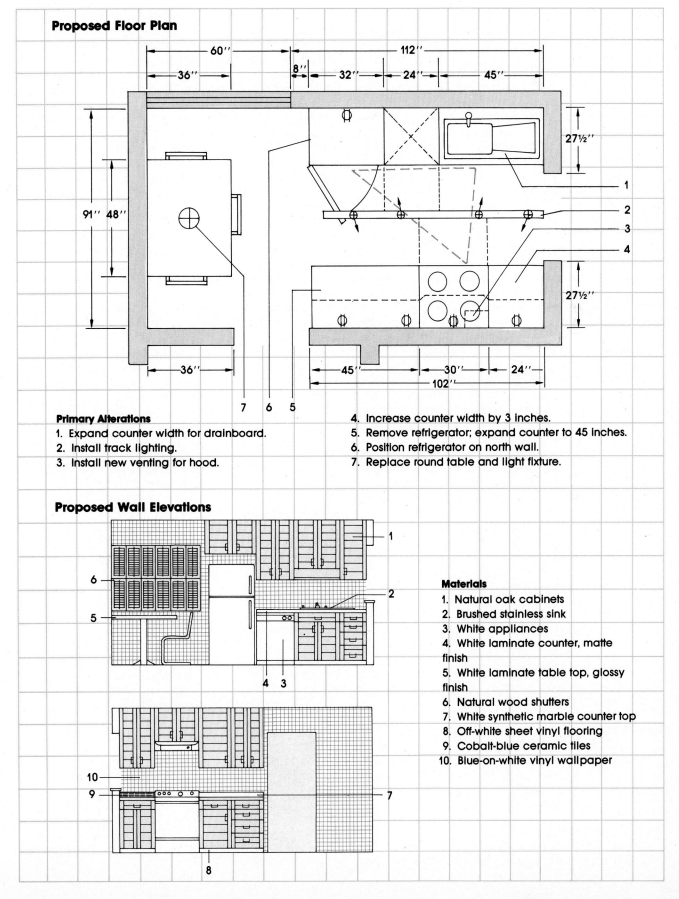

Proposed Floor Plan

Primary Alterations
1. Expand counter width for drainboard.
2. Install track lighting.
3. Install new venting for hood.

4. Increase counter width by 3 inches.
5. Remove refrigerator; expand counter to 45 inches.
6. Position refrigerator on north wall.
7. Replace round table and light fixture.

Proposed Wall Elevations

Materials
1. Natural oak cabinets
2. Brushed stainless sink
3. White appliances
4. White laminate counter, matte finish
5. White laminate table top, glossy finish
6. Natural wood shutters
7. White synthetic marble counter top
8. Off-white sheet vinyl flooring
9. Cobalt-blue ceramic tiles
10. Blue-on-white vinyl wallpaper

SCHEDULES & CONTRACTS

Schedules

Professional contractors with years of experience in this field rarely start hands-on work on a remodeling job until they have everything in hand. Although they know they will have to make extra stops, they try to avoid this. So go down your list of materials and determine which items will take the longest to get. For instance, if shipped from another state, cabinets might take eight weeks or more. Leave a margin for error or for late items. Decide which items you'll need first and make sure you order them earlier than products you might not need until later. Don't think "ship in eight weeks" means a firm date. This could mean only "ready to ship." To avoid delivery delays, ask for precise estimates of the dates you will have items in hand.

Installation dates. Draw up a rough estimate of the installation schedule. Determine which step will have to come first, which second, and so forth. For instance, a tiled counter will go in before a self-rimming stainless sink, but after a recessed porcelain sink. A tile or hardwood floor might go in before the cabinets, but a vinyl tile or sheet flooring will go in after the cabinets. Naturally, each step will vary in length. Ask the various installers how long they will take to accomplish their tasks, or estimate your own time for doing it. Plot all this out on a calendar and see which weeks you will have to hang around the house waiting for deliveries and which weeks you'll be working. Always allow some flexibility. Some kitchens can be installed in a few days. Others have been known to take weeks or months longer than scheduled. But you can try to get some sort of agreement among your various professionals as to when you should expect certain things to happen. Some of these dates will become part of any contract you draw up.

Temporary warehouse. Get some space ready in which to store the items that will be delivered—wrapped-up cabinets, cartons containing sink and faucets, and boxes of hardware. Store them so you have access to what you will need first.

Check every delivered item. Check out each item and inspect every piece of equipment to be sure you have received the correct model number, style, color, finish, size, and quantity. And make sure everything is in working condition and undamaged. It is frustrating to receive a cracked sink, but it is far worse if you don't discover this until you are about to put it in place. When you are satisfied that you have received the correct item and that it is ready to install, repack it and put it away.

Contracts

No matter what the size of your project or how much you trust the professionals you have chosen, it is wise to write up a contract. A written contract will ensure that all the terms you have agreed upon will be remembered, acted upon, and fulfilled.

Work Arrangements

There are many ways to work with a contractor but they generally fall into two main categories: Total Price, and Time and Materials.

Total Price. A total-price arrangement means the contractor charges you a bottom-line figure that includes everything. It can be one amount for the entire project or individual amounts for separate phases of the project. The advantage of this approach is that you know how much the job is going to cost before you start. The disadvantage is that the total will include a hidden markup—as much as 25 percent—to cover unforeseen problems. This is not refunded even if the job goes smoothly.

Time and Materials. A time and materials arrangement means that the contractor charges you an hourly rate for labor, the cost of materials, and a standard markup (usually 15 percent) for overhead and profit. The advantage of this approach is that you pay only for what you get. Your invoice clearly shows the amount of time worked, the cost of materials, and the markup. The disadvantage is that you don't know exactly how much the remodeling will cost until it is finished.

If you work on a time and materials basis, make sure you are clear about what the 15 percent markup includes and what it doesn't. For example, if you do the running around and pick up the materials but charge them to the contractor's account, will you still pay the markup fee? If you pay for C.O.D. materials ordered by the contractor, are they subject to the markup? Is consultation time charged separately or is it included in the overhead amount? Will workers supply all necessary tools or will you be charged a rental fee? Are plans included in the markup? Does the overhead figure cover the cost of replacing faulty materials discovered six months after the remodeling has been completed? Try to think of all the gray areas and make sure that they are understood and agreed upon by both of you.

Contract Forms

Most professionals have forms of their own. Some of these may say "Proposal" at the top. This is fine for an estimate, but should you ever find yourself in a legal dispute, a signed proposal is not a binding contract. Even if you must change the heading, make sure you sign a contract, not a proposal. Although the language used on some forms may sound overly legalistic to you, it has probably been worked out to protect the professional. It may even follow an industry standard drafted by the professional's trade organization. You can request explanations of any parts you don't readily understand; you can attach supplemental sheets written in your own words, indicating that the attachments are to be included as part of the contract signed; or you can decide to write your own contract.

Points to Cover in a Contract

No matter what form you use, any contract should include:

☐ a complete list of jobs to be performed and who will do them

☐ a complete list of materials and fixtures to be installed, who will purchase what, and delivery dates where possible

☐ starting date(s) for the project(s)

□ completion date(s) for the project(s)
□ a list of liability provisions, including liens, and warranties on work or materials
□ an outline of how changes in plan will be handled
□ a schedule of payments

Jobs to be performed. If the professional will be covering all phases of the project, then all steps should be spelled out in the contract. Your list will vary, of course, depending on your particular remodeling job, and on how much work you plan to do yourself. If you are working with several subcontractors, you may have several contracts, each spelling out only those jobs that will be performed by that particular contractor. Determine who is responsible for supplying the building department with the correct documentation, for buying the necessary permits, and for arranging for inspections. Dealing with the building department can be time consuming, so if your time is short or if your project is quite complex, you may prefer to let the contractor do this.

Materials and fixtures. All your materials will be specified on your final materials list, but there may be some you want to spell out in the contract as well, particularly if the professional will be ordering them. Specify materials in the same detail provided on your materials list. If you are having cabinets custom-built, you may want even more detail. Be sure it is clearly understood (in writing) who will purchase the materials, who is responsible for making sure deliveries are made, and to whom these materials will be charged.

Starting dates. You can't hold the professional responsible for late delivery on materials ordered, and it may be wise to schedule everything after delivery of all materials. The relevant portions of your contract might read something like this: "Dismantling to start on February 25, 19____, or upon delivery of (brand-name) cabinets and (brand-name) tiles."

Completion dates. These can be a bit trickier, so the terms should be clearly understood. "Days" can make a work period sound a lot shorter than it actually is. A contractor may work only four days a week, or may take off rainy or snowy days, holidays, vacations, and sick days. One family did not understand this and was unpleasantly surprised when a "90-day" contract actually took six months. Include some approximate dates by which certain phases of the project will be completed. If your contractor won't agree to include deadlines, try to find out why. Professionals should have a fairly good idea of how many days a job will take, and they can always add a "fudge factor" to cover any unforeseen difficulties. If you can only agree on an approximate completion date, include a clause stating that someone will be working on the job every day.

You can also insert a penalty clause specifying the amount of money to be deducted from the final payment for each day or week that work continues past the deadline date. If the contractor won't agree to such terms but you know from your reference-checking that he is responsible about deadlines and finishes jobs on time, you may not wish to pursue the penalty clause.

Special conditions and provisions. Hopefully you won't have a fire that destroys all the lumber that was just delivered, but you should be prepared for unforeseen problems and accidents. If you should have a fire, who is reponsible for replacing the damaged items? Ask your contractor for certificates of insurance. If he does not carry any, you can buy your own for the duration of the project. Make sure the contractor carries workman's compensation—this is his responsibility.

You can also spell out any other special conditions you want. For instance, you may wish to stipulate that you will not be responsible for liens against the contractor arising from the contract. This would protect you from being responsible for bills unpaid by the contractor. Warranties on the work should also appear in this section of the contract. You may wish to have a one-year warranty on the remodeling that includes free repairs and coverage for additional damage due to faulty materials or negligence. For instance, if a water heater is installed incorrectly and causes a fire or flood, you want to ensure that the contractor will repair or replace the hot water heater and repair any other areas of damage—at no cost to you.

It may be difficult to secure such terms in your contract. If you are willing to put out the money for highly reputable firms that have been in business for many years, you may be able to order the contract your way and feel confident it will be strictly followed.

Changes are the most common cause of misunderstanding and dissatisfaction. However carefully you have thought through your project, there are bound to be things you didn't think of and things you want to change when you actually see them. Be sure to agree in advance on how you will handle any changes in plans. This is especially important if you are working on a total-price basis: The smallest change can release the contractor from the original agreement. One method of dealing with such situations is to agree to make formal mini-contracts for each change as it comes up. There will be few disputes if everything is down on paper.

Payment schedules. Payments vary according to hourly or flat fee rates and the type of professional with whom you are working. However, you can generally expect to pay in stages. You might make a first payment early in the ordering or designing process, a second at the time materials are delivered or installed, and a final payment upon your acceptance of the finishing work. You may want the contract to specify the exact time that the final payment comes due: "Final payment of $X,XXX will be due 30 days after completion and acceptance of the work." The "acceptance" may be your only leverage if the contractor will not put in a clause stipulating penalty payments for late completion. If there are things not yet completed to your satisfaction, you can withhold this final payment until you are satisfied.

Don't be put off by the effort it may take to arrive at a sound contract. You don't need a contract that runs on for endless pages, but make sure both you and the professional understand and agree to all aspects of the project.

DISMANTLING THE OLD KITCHEN

To prepare your kitchen space
for its new look, you may need to take out the
old cabinets, flooring, and wall surfaces.
The illustrated instructions in this
chapter will show you how to strip
your kitchen down to its shell.

If you're simply replacing appliances, dismantling your kitchen is not very extensive. But if you're practically starting from scratch, dismantling is a project in itself. Whatever you do, removal generally occurs in the following order: appliances, counter tops, cabinets, flooring, lighting and other fixtures, wiring, plumbing, and structural elements; then prepare the space for installations. Read the sections in this chapter to get an idea of the amount of time the various procedures will entail.

Create a temporary kitchen. Unless your remodeling job will be quick and easy, you should think about setting up a temporary kitchen. Choose a work space that will limit the amount of inconvenience you'll have to endure. You'll need to keep foods cold, heat water, warm up dinners, or make sandwiches and salads. Try to find a work space that can include your old refrigerator. You'll also find it much easier to operate if you can set up your temporary kitchen near a laundry sink, bathroom, washbasin, or wet-bar sink. Easy access to water will simplify everything. If there is power, set up crock pots, skillets, and toasters. A microwave oven might handle most of the cooking chores, so if you're planning to buy one for your new kitchen, consider making the purchase early. You might also think about borrowing a recreational vehicle from a friend or neighbor.

When you're remodeling an older kitchen, you don't have to remove everything. Here, old cabinets are given a fresh coat of white paint, setting them off against the warm, dark wall color used to visually reduce the size of the room. The huge space above the cabinets, which could be seen as a big problem, is used to display a unique collection of basketry. White trim and contemporary blinds incorporate the old window into the design, and new tiles in a rustic style blend with the home's older character.

Box up everything you're not planning to use in your temporary kitchen, mark the contents of each carton, and store the boxes in a convenient place. Think ahead and anticipate the discomforts before they surprise you. With a little planning, some minor inconvenience, and a lot of good humor, you'll get through.

Prepare for the refuse. Make arrangements to get rid of any refuse. You may have to rent a dumpster or arrange to use a friend's truck to cart some of the rubbish to the dump, but you do want to make some sort of plan to collect and remove the debris. If you're planning to donate some items to charity, arrange for pickup. Find a place away from the kitchen to gather items for disposal so they won't clutter up your working area or get damaged.

Turn off utility lines. Before you work on any appliances, turn off your utility lines. If you don't have shutoff valves, you may have to turn off the main valve, disconnect plumbing fixtures, cap the pipes, and turn the water back on. Caps are measured by the pipe's inside diameter, and must be made of the same material as the pipe. They can be threaded, unthreaded, or plastic. Be sure to get the right type. Disconnect fuses or turn off circuits to the areas in which you're working. If you're uncertain, turn off all the power or get professional assistance. Your main gas valve is usually located near the gas meter. If you don't know how to turn it off, get help.

Because appliances, cabinets, and all surface coverings vary from house to house and in the method of installation, you may find variations between instructions here and your particular situation. Use these instructions as a guide and follow your own common sense. Whenever something is not clear to you or you feel uncertain about a procedure, seek advice. What you're trying to accomplish during the dismantling phase is a smooth, clean space which can accept all the new elements you want to install.

For a major project all of the appliances may have to be removed. If this is the case, or if anything more than the refrigerator is being relocated or coming out, determine what power or fuel systems will have to be disconnected, and turn off all power and gas. Shut off the main power switch or the kitchen circuit breakers before you start to work. And, if you will be working for quite some time, tape over the circuit breakers so they won't be turned on inadvertently. If you're not sure which circuit breakers control which areas of the house, turn them all off. Don't take chances. Turn off the main gas valve or propane connection if you are unsure how to turn off individual gas appliances. But be forewarned that once you turn off the gas to the whole house, all pilot lights will have to be relit before other appliances, like the hot water heater, will work again. As it is wise to have the utility company check over the line before you turn it back on, you may not want to do this more than once.

Freestanding electric range. Ease the appliance out from the back wall far enough to reach the thick pigtail plug behind it, and pull the plug from the wall. Then, pull the unit out into the kitchen area, put it on a dolly, and move it to the spot you have chosen. For a freestanding range with an upper oven and fan, disengage the duct connections first (see Removing a Hood/Vent on the facing page). Then, follow the simple steps for removing a freestanding range. Get help to move it out and away, since it will be heavier and more unwieldy than other types of ranges.

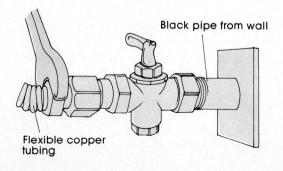

Hood and fan

Slide unit out

Drop-in range. Detach the unit from the base cabinets or the sides of flanking cabinets. You will see the fasteners when you open the oven door. It may also be attached to the side cabinets. Get someone to help you lift it out far enough to unplug or turn it off and disengage the gas valve. Then lift it onto a dolly.

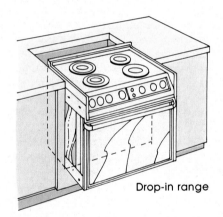

Drop-in range

Gas range. Move the unit just far enough forward to reach its gas shutoff valve. The flexible tubing should give you a couple of feet. Turn the valve toward "off" until it's tight. Be sure you understand exactly how to go about this or have someone with you who does. Disconnect the flexible tubing from the gas valve with a small wrench. Then slide the range out of its position and move it out of the kitchen area. If you do not plan to reuse the gas line, disconnect the supply line. With the main gas valve off, remove the supply line valve and put a plug fitting over the gas pipe inside the stud wall. After that you can ask the utility company to check the system and relight the pilot lights for all your gas appliances.

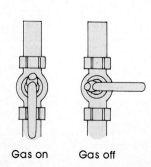

Black pipe from wall

Flexible copper tubing

Gas on   Gas off

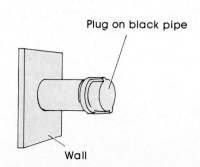

Plug on black pipe

Wall

Wall ovens. The electrical or gas connections are probably in the cabinet below the unit. Unplug the cord from the wall socket or turn off the gas valve. Detach the gas connection. Open oven doors to see the screws that hold the unit to framework or cabinetry. Unscrew the fasteners and ease the unit forward in its cabinet until you can lift it down onto a dolly.

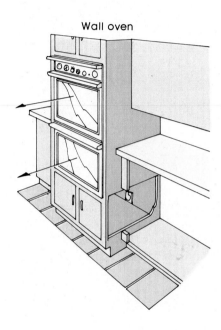

Wall oven

Cooktops. The power cord or gas valve for cooktops will probably be in the cabinet below or to one side. Unplug the cord or turn off the valve and disconnect the flexible tubing from the valve. Then unscrew the fasteners that hold the

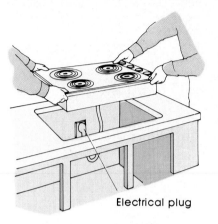

Electrical plug

unit to the counter top. Lift up the unit and remove it. If you don't plan to use the gas valve again, disconnect the supply line (as described on page 66 for a gas range).

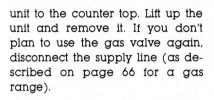

Gas shutoff

Barbecue cooktop. A barbecue cooktop with a downvent will have a vent system inside the base cabinet that goes through the floor or through the wall. Disconnect the unit from the duct the same way you do for a hood vent (see below). Detach the mountings and lift the unit out.

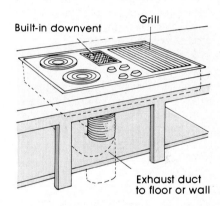

Built-in downvent

Grill

Exhaust duct to floor or wall

Removing a Hood/Vent

1. After making sure the electricity is off, disconnect the wiring. You will probably find the electrical connection beneath the easily removable light diffuser or filter panel. Disconnect the wires, and cap those coming from the wall. Keep any pairs of wires together, and cap each single wire separately. The bare copper wire is the ground and needs no cap.

2. Open the cabinet doors above the hood to see how the vent connects to the duct. If you find a round metal collar, unsnap it. If you find a band of silver tape around flexible ducting, disconnect the unit by stripping off the tape. Or you may find flanges that hold down a sheet metal box custom made to fit your hood-to-duct configuration. Pull up the nails or remove the screws holding the flanges.

3. Look up inside the hood to see where it is attached to the upper cabinets. Remove these screws from mounting brackets or holes and lift the hood out and down.

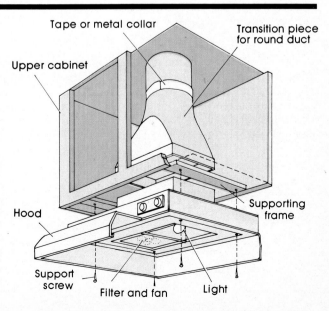

Tape or metal collar

Upper cabinet

Transition piece for round duct

Hood

Supporting frame

Support screw

Filter and fan

Light

Refrigerator

1. Remove food, empty the freezer compartment, and then pull the unit away from the wall as far as you can while it is still connected.

2. Pull the plug or turn off the gas connection where the flexible tube connects with the black gas pipe. If you have had little experience working with gas, have the utility company do this job for you.

3. Unplumb the icemaker by following the small copper tube out the back to its shutoff valve next to the floor or near the sink. Turn off the faucet or small tap on the cold water line. Then, using pliers or a wrench, turn the brass nuts on the compression rings that attach the tube to the faucet or valve until the tube comes free. Some water may spill out of it, but not enough to harm anything. Tape the extending tube to the side of the refrigerator.

4. Put the refrigerator on rollers, and move it to your temporary kitchen or storage area. If you're storing it, be sure to cover its surface and tie it shut.

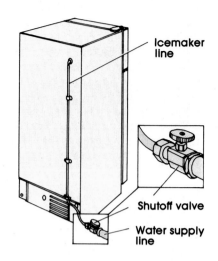

Icemaker line

Shutoff valve

Water supply line

Dishwasher

1. Look under the sink to see if the dishwasher connections have been threaded through holes in the sides of the cabinet. You should see a small copper pipe to the water line, a black rubber pipe to either the air gap or the disposal, and a cord to an electric plug. If you do not find them, look for any mounting brackets at floor level on either side of the dishwasher and disconnect them. Then grasp the dishwasher by the top lip or the bottom frame, and move it forward slowly, pulling hard, until you can get behind it to work.

2. Disconnect the plug from the outlet. In most places it's illegal to wire the dishwasher directly; if yours was wired, turn off the power and disconnect the wires from their junction box at the wall, capping the wires that remain in the wall.

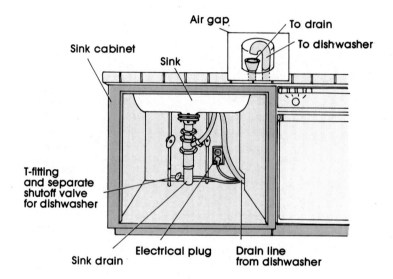

Air gap

To drain

To dishwasher

Sink cabinet

Sink

T-fitting and separate shutoff valve for dishwasher

Electrical plug

Drain line from dishwasher

Sink drain

3. Shut off the water at the shutoff valve. Detach the black rubber hose at the air gap, the waste fitting, or the collar of the garbage disposal. Disconnect this wasteline connection from the plumbing system by loosening the screw clamps on the hose fittings or unthreading the pipe fitting. You need not detach the hose from the dishwasher; simply feed it back through the cabinet sides to the back of the dishwasher. Then, pull the unit forward, put it on a dolly, and transport it to your temporary warehouse for storage or removal. If you plan to reuse it, tape a cover over the door for protection.

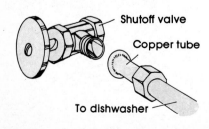

Shutoff valve

Copper tube

To dishwasher

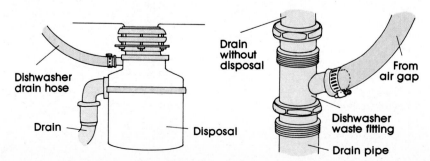

Dishwasher drain hose

Drain

Disposal

Drain without disposal

From air gap

Dishwasher waste fitting

Drain pipe

Garbage Disposal and Sink

1. Turn off the electric circuit to which your garbage disposal unit is connected. Shut off the water supply lines at the shutoff valves below the sink. If you don't have these, turn off the main valve near the front of the house. Then disconnect the fittings at the sink and cap them. You can get caps at any plumbing supply or hardware store. Be sure to get caps of the right size and proper threading that are made of the same metal as your pipes. With pipes capped, turn on the main valve again to restore water to the rest of the house.

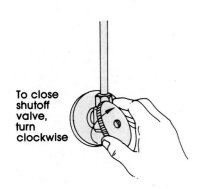

To close shutoff valve, turn clockwise

2. Disconnect the trap. Have a bucket handy to catch the water that stands in the trap. With a pipe wrench that will handle 1- to 1½-inch pipe, or with a large set of channel locks, disconnect the chrome fittings between the garbage disposal or the sink and the P-trap. Remove the trap.

Disconnect the trap

Disposal

Bucket to catch water

3. Disconnect the garbage disposal. Pull the plug from the socket. (In most places, it is illegal to wire the garbage disposal unit directly, but if yours is presently wired, turn off the power, disconnect the wires from the box in the wall, and cap them.) If you have a dishwasher or an air gap, you should have already disconnected its black drain hose. Unscrew the three tension screws that hold the garbage disposal against the bottom of the sink or unclasp the snap ring and rubber sleeve. Drop the whole unit down and remove it. Store it with the P-trap.

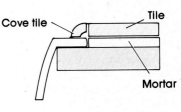

Tension screws

Drain hose from dishwasher or air gap

Plug

4. Disconnect the water supply lines. Open the sink faucets to let water drain down into the supply lines. Crawl into the cabinet under the sink and locate the nut that connects the faucet lines to the hot and cold supply lines. Loosen and disconnect the nuts that hold the faucet to the sink. Pull out the faucet from above. Store with nut and copper or chrome connections.

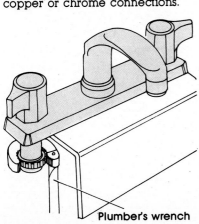

Plumber's wrench

5. Disconnect the sink. The sequence for removing your sink will vary, depending on the type of counter top and sink installation you have. If your sink is recessed under tiles you will have to remove some of these tiles first. Then you can take out the entire counter-top unit (not just the finish material) as one piece. If you have a stainless self-rimming sink (one with a top flange) or a surface-mounted sink (one with a separate steel rim around it), you will find small clips underneath the counter top. Loosen these with a screwdriver until you can jiggle them free. Lift out the sink. If you have a self-rimming porcelain sink, you will only have to pry it loose from the adhesive and lift it out. A cast-iron sink is always much heavier than other types, so you will need someone standing by to give you a hand when you remove it.

Cove tile

Tile

Mortar

Recessed Sink

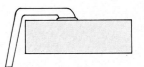

Self-Rimming Porcelain Sink

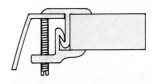

Surface-Mounted Steel Rim Sink

COUNTER TOPS

Most counter tops are merely pieces of plywood nailed or screwed to the base cabinets with a finish surface glued or laid on top. The only part worth saving is the finish surface—not even that if it is plastic laminate.

Obviously, you will need to remove the sink and fittings before you can take out the counter top, and you may have to remove all the doors and drawers to get to the fasteners.

Tiles. Tiles are mostly glass, and broken bits can fly everywhere. Always wear gloves and goggles, and, if dust bothers you, wear a respirator or gauze mask. Whether you can get tiles out in one piece will depend on how gentle you are and how firmly they are attached. Unless the tile is special, don't bother.

1. Remove any wood trim with a hammer and prybar.
2. Score or break the grout using a hammer and cold (brick) chisel. Then, working from the edges toward the center, tap the chisel or flat-nosed prybar to get under the

bottom of the tile, which may be glued down or embedded in mortar. Free as many edges as you can before gently prying the tile out. Clean out all surrounding grout. If the tile breaks, clean out all the pieces, knock out surrounding grout, and try the next one.

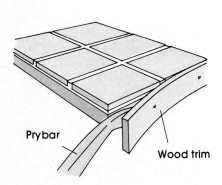

Prybar

Wood trim

Cold chisel

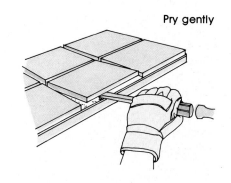

Pry gently

Plastic laminate counters and wood slabs. These two types of counter tops are usually screwed or nailed to the base cabinets. Locate the fastenings by looking up inside the cabinet, and then remove them. If the tops are also glued to the cabinets, break the seal as illustrated in the section on synthetic marble slabs on this page. Because wood is not as brittle as synthetic marble, you can probably use a prybar.

Synthetic marble slabs. These are normally glued to the plywood base and may snap if you just pry them off. Ease a putty knife between the slab and the base to create as large and long a crack as possible. Use any appropriate tool to break the seal as much and

as far in as you can reach. If you know what type of glue was used, try squirting an appropriate solvent into the crack you have made. Try to rock the slab and break the remaining seal or gently pry it off.

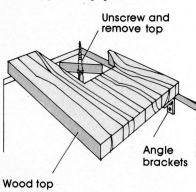

Unscrew and remove top

Wood top

Angle brackets

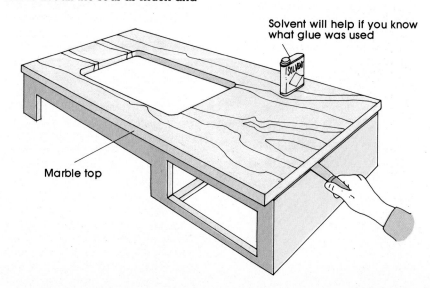

Solvent will help if you know what glue was used

Marble top

REMOVING
CABINETS

Cabinets can be attached in several different combinations: nailed or screwed to the wall, to the soffit above, to each other, hung on metal or wood cabinet hangers, or built into the wall structure. The age and type of your cabinets will determine some of the specific steps for their removal. Older cabinets are sometimes built into the wall itself, as part of the structure, and you may have to demolish them and part of the wall. You can take them apart with your hammer, prybar, and a saw, and save the lumber. Metal cabinets are attached to the wall on hangers. Simply lift them out and away from the wall at the bottoms, then lift them off the hangers. Remove the hangers from the wall.

Except in these cases, you and your helper(s) will take out the wall units first, resting them on the base units as you take them down. After the wall units have been taken away, you'll take out the base cabinets. Take off all the doors and remove all drawers. If you plan to save the hardware for any reason, store all the pulls and knobs and their screws in plastic bags.

Wall cabinets. Look inside the cabinets to see whether they are attached to the soffit with screws. If so, remove them. Then check to see whether screws or nails were used to secure the cabinets to the wall. If screws were used, remove them. If nails were used, slip a flat prybar between the back of the unit and the wall—at both the top and the bottom—and pry it loose, having someone brace the cabinet from below. Put a wood block between your prybar and the wall surface so you don't gouge the wallboard or plaster. If nails won't loosen, use a hammer to pound the cabinet toward the wall. This will force the nail heads to protrude so you can draw them out. If cabinets are also attached to each other, you can lower the whole line onto the base cabinets with a helper or you can detach the individual cabinets and lift them down separately.

Base cabinets. The lower units will be attached to the wall at the top— with nails if they are older or cheaper types, with screws if they are newer, more substantial types. Pry them loose or unscrew them. Cut the cove molding at the floor with a knife, or remove the baseboard, rubber base, or molding by prying it away with your prybar, hammer end, or chisel. Remove any nails. Lift the cabinets out of place and remove them from the area.

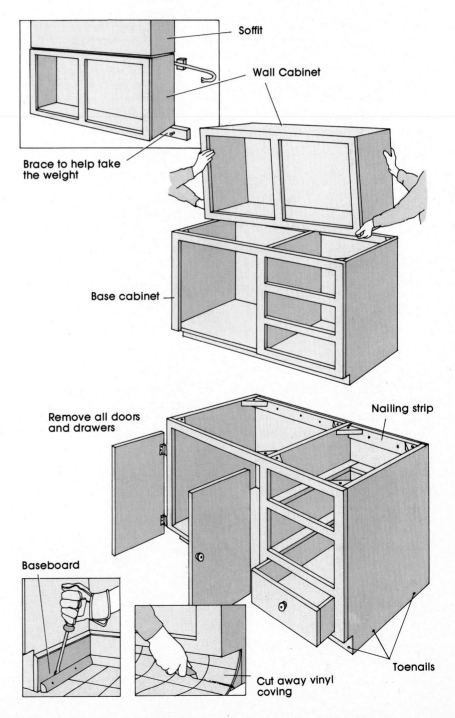

Soffit

Wall Cabinet

Brace to help take the weight

Base cabinet

Remove all doors and drawers

Nailing strip

Baseboard

Cut away vinyl coving

Toenails

WALL COVERINGS

Depending on how extensive your remodeling project is, you may want to remove all your present wall and ceiling surfaces. This is not a particularly complicated job, but it can be time consuming and messy. Wear appropriate protective clothing, and try to avoid totally demolishing subsurfaces unless that is your intent. If you're removing surface materials around light fixtures, you may need to remove the fixtures now (see page 74).

Trims and moldings. Before you can begin to take off any wall coverings, you must remove all trim and molding. If you plan to reuse them—older style moldings can be expensive—pry them loose very gently. Tap them back to loosen and withdraw nails or drive nails through. Mark or number them and draw a little map so you know where they go before storing them. If they have layers of paint and stains on them, you may want to strip them while they are loose.

Wallpaper. If you have two or more layers of wallpaper under your present surface, you're better off renting a steamer or having someone come in with one. For a single layer or so, purchase a bottle of wallpaper remover. Spray sections of the paper, let the solution set, respray, and simply peel off with a wide putty knife. Then sluice down the wall with a sponge and a weak solution of TSP (trisodium phosphate), rinse, and let dry. Sand any uneven areas.

Paneling. Pry loose and pull off wood or hardboard paneling. Panels that are glued on may pull away hunks of plaster or wallboard. Replace or patch these sections of wall. If you plan to save the wood or hardboard paneling, pry it very gently until you can get it to come away in an unbroken piece. You may have to drive the nails clear through in order to free the panels. Use a countersink punch for this. Then mark and clean them before you store them.

Wood wedges

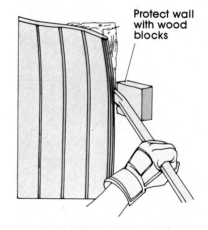

Protect wall with wood blocks

Ceramic tiles. If you want to save some of the tiles, carefully chisel away all grout and gently pry up the tiles. Otherwise, bang, break, and pry, then scrape the broken mess away. Don't forget your protective eyewear and gloves. Older tiled walls may have chicken wire

and mud on lath underneath. Insert your prybar under the chicken wire to get up large chunks. Newer installations may have only mastic behind the tiles, which is less difficult to scrape away than mortar. After removing all the tiles, patch and repair the surface.

Acoustical tile ceiling. Acoustical tiles may be glued or nailed to the ceiling or hung on a metal gridwork. Pry off glued or nailed tiles with your handy prybar. Lift suspended tiles out of the gridwork, then unscrew the metal frame and detach it.

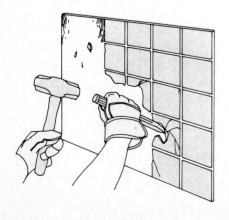

Mud, chicken wire, and lath

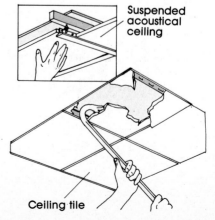

Suspended acoustical ceiling

Ceiling tile

FLOOR SURFACES

If you plan to install a new floor surface and you have only one layer of existing flooring material, you may be able to lay the new surface right over the old one. Wood and vinyl can be placed over an old vinyl floor, for example, but vinyl cannot be placed over ceramic tile—the uneven surface of the tiles will show through. Your old vinyl floor must be smooth and even enough to allow a secure bond between it and the new flooring. It should not be damaged and should be free of old wax, polish, dirt, and glue. It is also possible to lay a new subfloor of ⅜-inch particleboard directly on top of your existing flooring (see page 75). However, if your present flooring material is badly cracked or damaged or consists of several layers and you do not want to put down an entirely new subfloor, you should remove what is there now. To do so, follow the steps below.

Sheet vinyl. Remove baseboard or rubber molding. Pry off tacked-on caps of cove molding strips or cut coving. Grab a corner of the vinyl and pull it out and up. If necessary, pull hard, but pull smoothly. It may tear or leave backing stuck to the floor, but just keep working it away from the floor. In some cases it may be easiest to cut the vinyl into strips and pull up one strip at a time. Or you can move across the room or work from all four corners toward the center to get the vinyl up in one sheet. Remove the glue with a putty knife or floor scraper, a little hoe-like tool. Rent one if you have a large floor area to do.

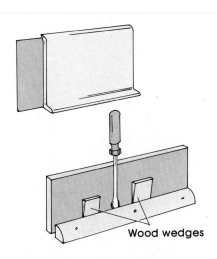

Wood wedges

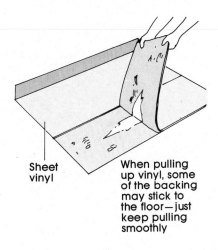

Sheet vinyl

When pulling up vinyl, some of the backing may stick to the floor—just keep pulling smoothly

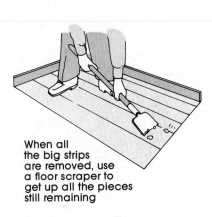

When all the big strips are removed, use a floor scraper to get up all the pieces still remaining

Vinyl tiles. Remove edge moldings or baseboards. Pry up tiles with a 6-inch putty knife. Scrape off the glue as described above for sheet vinyl.

Vinyl-asbestos tiles. These old black tiles have to be warmed with a propane torch before they are soft enough to lift up with a putty knife. You can rent the equipment to do it yourself or have someone else do this time-consuming and messy job. Cleanup is done with acetone on a rag. Because acetone is a highly volatile solvent, open windows, make sure there is plenty of cross ventilation, and don't smoke.

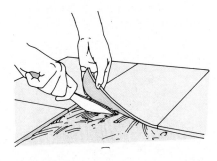

If you can't remove old glue with a scraper, you may need to use a solvent

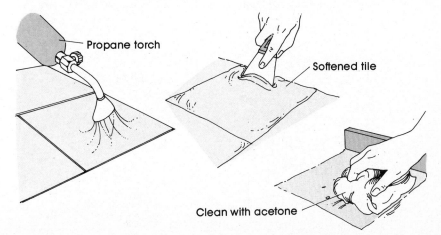

Propane torch

Softened tile

Clean with acetone

LIGHT FIXTURES

If you are planning to put your new light fixtures in the same locations as the old ones, you can remove the old fixtures now or wait until the new kitchen elements are installed, using the old fixtures as sources of light for working. You'll need only to disconnect the lights long enough to paint or paper and install the new fixtures. If you plan structural changes or rewiring, remove them now. Turn off the fixtures and fuses or circuit breakers leading to the kitchen area, remove bulbs and fluorescent tubes, and then remove the fixtures as shown in Steps 1 and 2 below. If you are going to keep switches and outlets in their present locations, simply unscrew and remove the plates and save them. If you're removing or relocating them, follow Step 3.

1. Wall lights. Unscrew the mounting nut or nuts on the wall plates, and lift the fixture plates away from the wall. Detach any fixture mountings behind the plate. Disconnect the fixture wires from those in the wall, and cap those remaining in the wall.

2. Ceiling lights. Unscrew the nuts holding up the ceiling plates. If there is a center post, unscrew it or unscrew the bracket holding the fixtures. Lift the unit away and have someone hold it while you work.

Disconnect the wires and cap those remaining in the ceiling, tucking them back up into the hole. Keep all the parts of the wall or ceiling light fixtures together if you plan to reuse them.

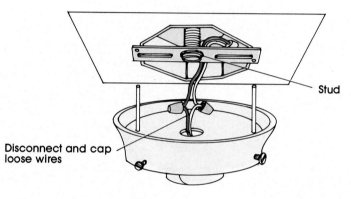

Stud

Disconnect and cap
loose wires

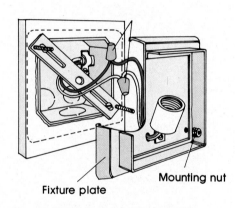

Fixture plate

Mounting nut

3. Switches and receptacles. With the power off, remove the face plate. Then remove the screws that hold the switch or outlet to the box. Pull the unit out, and disconnect the wires. Pry loose or unscrew the mounting box from the stud. Unscrew the cable connection at the back of the box, pull the wires out through the hole in the box, and remove the box. Trace the cable back to the nearest junction box, and remove the cover. If the new switch or outlet will not be in this area, disconnect the wires in the junction box, cap those remaining in the box, and pull the cable out of the wall. If you plan to move the new outlet or switch closer to the junction box, cut the cable to the appropriate length, leaving it attached at the junction box, and reattach the mounting box, wires, and switch or outlet in the new location. If you plan to move the switch or outlet farther from the junction box, run a longer length of cable from the box to the new location, drilling holes through the studs between and attaching the wires at the junction box. Run the wires into the new box and attach them to the outlet or switch, and then mount the unit securely to the box. Install the plates when the wall surfaces are finished.

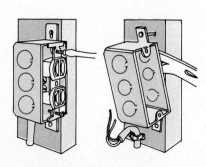

Disconnect wires and pry
box loose

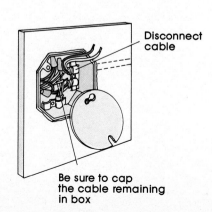

Disconnect
cable

Be sure to cap
the cable remaining
in box

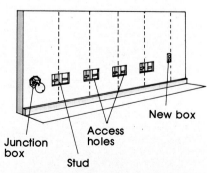

Disconnect
cable

New box

Access
holes

Junction
box

Stud

Use reeled wire to pull cable
through studs—patch wall later

PREPARING FOR INSTALLATION

After removing basic elements from the kitchen space, you may have some additional work to do to prepare for new installations. Clean up appliances that can be reused, and send them out for refinishing or repair if necessary. Professionals can spray on a new coat of enamel to match new appliances or just to change the color. If you plan to reuse cabinets, strip them and prepare them for their new finishes or trims. Sort and clean old tiles. You may be able to get the last tidbits of mortar off of the tiles by boiling them in a large pot. Do all your plumbing, wiring, or ducting work at this time. Then clean and repair all surfaces as described below.

1. Smoothing walls. Fill small holes with wallboard compound or spackle. Larger holes have to be stuffed first or the patching material will just fall through the hole; fine wire mesh is good for this. If you have gaping holes or the wall is covered with gouges, replace the entire surface with wallboard. If you want to tackle this yourself, refer to Ortho's book, *Basic Home Repairs.*

2. Smoothing floors. If you are planning to lay new flooring material directly on your existing floor surface, nail down any bumps or bulges, and smooth out buckled areas to create as smooth a surface as possible. Scrape off all glue and/or paint, and make sure there are no nail or screw heads sticking up. Using a putty knife, fill in dips or hollows or an embossed floor pattern with cement filler.

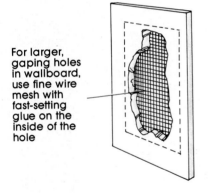

For larger, gaping holes in wallboard, use fine wire mesh with fast-setting glue on the inside of the hole

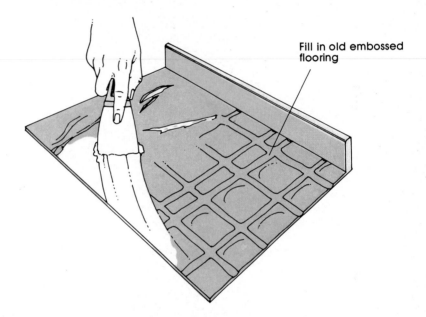

Fill in old embossed flooring

3. Repairing damaged floors. If any areas of your floor look damaged, particularly from water, you must repair them. Remove the surface material to expose the subfloor. If this is damaged, find a joist on either side of the damaged area in the same way you find studs. Then, using a circular saw set to the depth of your subfloor, cut a section to expose ¾ inch of each joist—this will give you something to nail your patch to. From a piece of plywood the same thickness as your existing subfloor, cut a patch to fit the hole exactly and nail it to the joists.

4. Installing a new subfloor. If all of the existing subfloor is in bad shape, lay a new one, either on top of your existing floor or directly to the joists. Lay sheets of plywood in a staggered pattern so that the joints do not form straight lines. Nail down the sheets. (For more details on installing a subfloor, see Ortho's book, *Basic Carpentry Techniques.*)

Replacement patch cut to size

¾ inch of joist showing

Joist

Subfloor

Nail patch into exposed joist

INSTALLING YOUR NEW KITCHEN

As you follow the step-by-step
illustrations in this chapter,
you'll watch your design come to life.
And when you begin using your new kitchen,
you'll have the pleasure of knowing
it was worth all the effort.

You're down to the last phase of your project—installation. Following your plan, you'll want to make sure all your structural changes are made and that new plumbing, wiring, gas, heat, and vent lines are in place. As mentioned elsewhere in this book, you will find step-by-step instructions for plumbing and wiring tasks in Ortho's books, *Basic Wiring Techniques* and *Basic Plumbing Techniques*. With your floors and walls patched and smoothed, follow the installation steps outlined in this chapter. If you want, make up a checklist of the tasks you need to do during installation, and put them in some sort of sequence so you can check them off as you go. That way, you will have an idea of what still lies ahead and how much time will be involved. The order of installation varies, but the following list represents the most common sequence:

☐ ceramic tile or hardwood floors
☐ wall cabinets
☐ base cabinets and islands
☐ cabinet doors, drawers, and hardware
☐ plywood base for tile counter tops
☐ recessed sinks
☐ counter tops—tile, marble, wood, etc.
☐ surface-mounted sinks and sink fittings

"Built-in" is the installation theme of this kitchen (also pictured on pages 34–35). A central island in the middle of the parquet floor is topped with a laminate counter trimmed in the same wood used on cabinetry, windowsills, and hood. Custom drawers and shelves of varying shapes provide generous storage on both exterior and interior walls. Because the kitchen has relatively little natural light, contemporary spot lights and hanging lanterns provide the room with balanced lighting.

☐ disposal
☐ dishwasher
☐ icemaker connections
☐ hood/vent
☐ cooktops
☐ wall ovens and microwaves
☐ vinyl flooring
☐ range
☐ refrigerators, freezers, and icemakers
☐ lighting fixtures
☐ decorative and finishing elements.

The two items you should note in particular are flooring and appliances. Ceramic tile and hardwood floors are laid before cabinets are installed, whereas vinyl flooring is laid after the cabinets are in place. The plumbing connections for icemakers and dishwashers are generally installed along with the sink, disposal, and dishwasher, but the other major appliances—ranges, refrigerators, and trash compactor—are installed last, after vinyl flooring has been laid.

In this book, instructions for installing all appliances are grouped together as are the floor installations. You can determine the order of your own tasks, but you should plan them according to the most efficient and logical sequence for your kitchen. If you have any questions, refer to the list on this page, or check with the professionals you're working with.

As mentioned on page 65 of Chapter Four, be sure to turn off your utility lines before you work on any appliances or connections. And bear in mind that instructions will vary according to the type, model, and style of the appliance or element you're installing. Use the instructions in this chapter as a guide, but always follow specific manufacturer's instructions whenever there are differences.

INSTALLING
CABINETS

Base and wall cabinets are installed in basically the same way, but it is easier to install the upper units first so you can get at them. Since they hang on the wall, they need to be very secure. Most cabinets—uppers and lowers—come with a scribe allowance at the edges, which meets the wall. This can be planed off so cabinets will be flush against the wall. If the cabinets don't have this scribe, you'll want to trim the edges with a small piece of molding. If cabinets go all the way to the ceiling, you'll want to trim that edge with molding, too.

1. Locate and mark wall studs with a light pencil line drawn from ceiling to floor. Use a board as a straightedge or drop a plumb line. Next, measure the height of the base cabinets and add to it the thickness of the counter top. Take this measurement up from the floor and draw a line across the wall to indicate where the top of the counter surface will touch. Use a board as a straightedge and a level to make sure it is precisely horizontal. Then mark the wall where the bottom of the upper units will rest, which is usually 18 or 19 inches above the counter surface. Draw a line across the wall, making sure it is parallel to the top of the base units. Attach a 1 by 2 ledger to the wall with the top of the board touching your line for the upper units. Nail it to the studs, and then mark the cabinet widths along its length.

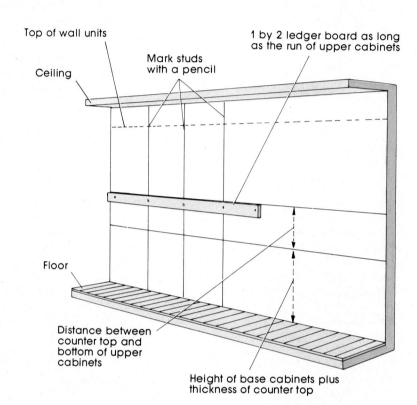

Top of wall units

Ceiling

Mark studs with a pencil

1 by 2 ledger board as long as the run of upper cabinets

Floor

Distance between counter top and bottom of upper cabinets

Height of base cabinets plus thickness of counter top

2. Make several jacks to support the wall cabinets while you put them in place. Nail wide blocks to each end of a 2 by 4. The total height of the jack should equal the distance from the floor to the bottom of the upper units. Put these jacks in position near the ledger.

Block

Ledger

Distance from floor to bottom of wall units

2 by 4

Wall

Block

3. Before you install the upper units, prepare any cabinets that will house a hood/vent or ducts. Place the cabinet upside down on the floor. Put the hood top on it—upside down and centered or positioned the way you want it. Mark the outline of the vent hole on the base of the cabinet. Drill a starter hole for your saw. Cut around the outline and remove the waste. Then make a paper pattern of the wall or ceiling where this cabinet will go, showing where the end of the duct will enter it. Place the pattern on the back or top of the cabinet and outline the duct hole. Cut this circle out of the cabinet. Install the cabinet along with all the other wall units as described in the following steps. To install the hood, see page 87.

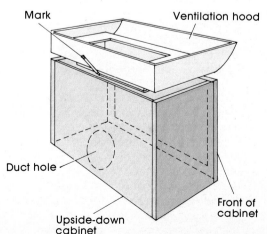

Mark

Ventilation hood

Duct hole

Upside-down cabinet

Front of cabinet

4. Mark the stud locations of the wall on the cabinet's hanging cleats, and drill pilot holes for screws. Take off the doors and lift out any loose items. Lift the first cabinet into position, resting it on the ledger and jacks. Check both level and plumb. If necessary, use shims at the back of the cabinet to bring the cabinet into plumb. Insert 2½-inch screws through the hanging cleat at the back of the cabinet into the studs. Attach all the other wall units the same way. Then screw adjacent units to each other. You may have to loosen wall screws to get the faces to line up. Recheck the level. Then remove the jacks and ledger board. Patch any holes in the wall when the base units are in place.

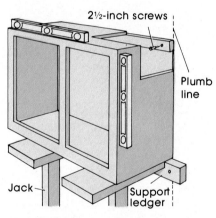

2½-inch screws

Plumb line

Jack

Support ledger

5. Next, set each base cabinet in place. If your cabinets come with separate bases, set the bases in position and level them, shimming where necessary and anchoring them to the floor. Then place the cabinet units on top of them. If you're planning to raise the counter height, nail 1 by 4s or 2 by 4s flat to the floor at the front and back edges of the cabinets, level them, and anchor them to the floor. Then set the base units on top of them, shimming where necessary to make them level. As you set base units in place, leave room for appliances. Be sure to check the actual dimensions of your appli-

ances, and then leave ¼ inch clearance—more if you're using end panels (see Step 6). Check the position of base units against the line on your wall. The tops should be below the line by the thickness of your counter top. Screw all adjacent units together and move your level along the entire bank of cabinets. Shim where necessary. Then check the plumb—the level from front to back. Again, shim where necessary. Attach the entire bank of units to the wall by inserting screws through the top support cleat of the cabinet frame and into the studs.

18 or 19″

Counter top—2″

Base unit—34″

Total height of base unit and counter top 36″

Base of wall cabinets

Floor

Base cabinets

6. When all your upper and lower units are secured, you can install any end panels ordered with the cabinets. These can box in the appliances on one or both sides or support a counter that ends over a dishwasher or compactor. Attach them to cabinets and floor with small L-brackets. Install shelves or drawer racks, drawer glides, and interior accessory items such as pullout racks or bins. Install door hinges if not already attached, and hang doors. Adjust them to get an even line across the entire run by loosening the hinge screws and sliding the hinge fractionally one way or the other. Tighten the screws and recheck the door.

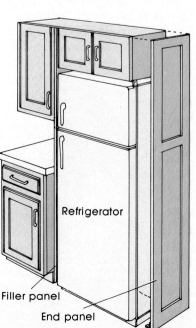

Refrigerator

Filler panel

End panel

7. To install kitchen island cabinets, screw individual units together and check for level and plumb on all four sides. Shim if necessary and screw to the floor. If the base is separate, you should fasten it to the floor, first using toe nails or angle brackets, then place and anchor the cabinets to the leveled base.

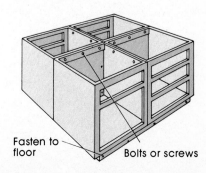

Fasten to floor

Bolts or screws

INSTALLING
COUNTER TOPS

If your cabinets are prefinished, you are ready to install the counter tops. If they are not, you should finish them first. Plastic laminate counter tops are best made by a professional and are simply fitted to the walls and screwed to the cabinets from underneath. You'll want to have the professional measure your space to ensure an exact fit. Ready-made, wood-block counter tops come with a wood backsplash that is screwed to the back edge of the top.

Wood counter tops used near the sink should be water-proofed on the top, bottom, and on all exposed sides (such as the sink cutout). You attach these in the same way you attach a plastic laminate counter—by screwing them to the cabinets from underneath. Marble and synthetic marble tops are also easily installed at this point—instructions are illustrated below. Tile counters require some additional preparation. See pages 82–83.

Synthetic Marble Counters

Some brands of synthetic marble, like Corian®, are available in slabs and are almost as easy to work with as wood. You can drill, saw, sand, and glue the material. If you make your own synthetic marble counter, you may have only one choice for the edge—the edge of the slab itself—which is ¼, ½, or ¾ inch thick, unless you have a router, in which case you'll be able to create a decorative front edge. You might also be able to cut a narrow strip and edge-glue it to give the illusion of a thicker slab. However, you will probably have to butt-join corners rather than miter them. If you wish to you can also trim the flat sides with wood.

1. Measure your counter area from end to end as well as from front to back. Include 1 inch or more for the front and side overhangs and 1 inch to cover any end panels. Make a plan of the counter, including the cutout for the sink (see page 84) and the backsplash or sidesplash pieces.

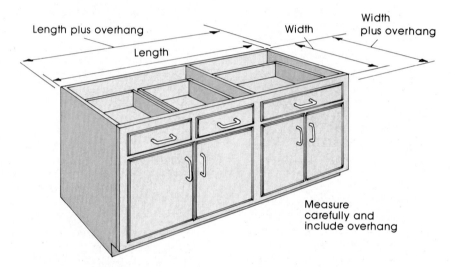

Length plus overhang
Length
Width
Width plus overhang

Measure carefully and include overhang

2. Cut both the counter top and backsplash pieces according to your measurements. Wear goggles to protect your eyes from flying particles. Then make the sink cutout as described on page 84.

3. Set the counter top in place and check both level and plumb. Make sure front trim pieces won't interfere with drawers or doors. If they do, trim them, or raise the counter top by placing plywood blocks every few inches all the way around the top of the cabinets. Nail the blocks down, replace the counter, and check the level again. If the counter is not level, add shims where necessary.

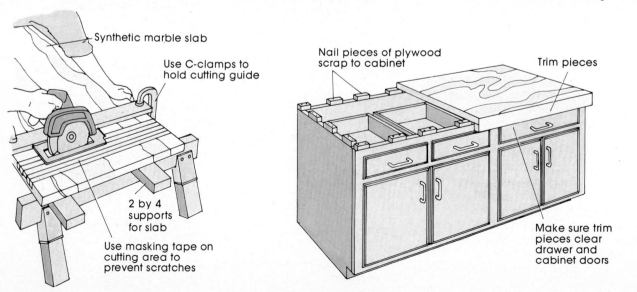

Synthetic marble slab

Use C-clamps to hold cutting guide

2 by 4 supports for slab

Use masking tape on cutting area to prevent scratches

Nail pieces of plywood scrap to cabinet

Trim pieces

Make sure trim pieces clear drawer and cabinet doors

4. Attach the trim pieces by turning the counter top over and gluing the front and side trim pieces to the underside of the counter, using a recommended glue. Clamp, and let the seal dry overnight. Then scrape off any remnants or remove them with a drop of acetone on a piece of cloth. Next, lay a bead of glue around the tops of the cabinets or plywood blocks. Place the counter in position, press down firmly, and let the glue dry. Finally, attach the backsplash to the counter, snugly against the wall, with the recommended adhesive. Seal the joints and seams with silicone. Wipe away any excess with a wet rag over your finger, forming a smooth concave seam. Seal the wall seam with silicone, and let it dry.

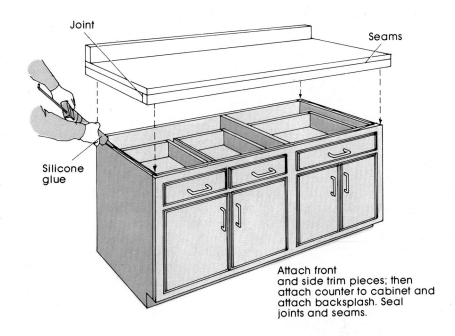

Joint

Seams

Silicone glue

Attach front and side trim pieces; then attach counter to cabinet and attach backsplash. Seal joints and seams.

Installing a Marble Counter Top

Natural marble has been used on counters and table tops for centuries. The cool surface makes it ideal for rolling out candies and pastry. Search antique stores or wreckers' yards for old pieces of marble, and adapt your kitchen counters to make use of your finds. Or, if there is a marble supplier in your area, have a piece custom cut and edged.

1. Measure the area for your marble top and backsplash carefully. If this area is at a lower level (for use as a baking center, for example), allow for side pieces where the counter returns to the standard height. These side pieces can be in a matching marble or any other appropriate material. Take these measurements to a marble dealer and have the pieces cut and edged.

2. Position counter, back, and end pieces to make sure they are even with other counter surfaces and backsplashes. If not, raise the marble slab or the surrounding counter top by nailing plywood blocks to the top frame of the base cabinets.

3. Glue the slab in place. This step may be unnecessary since marble is extremely heavy. However, if you want to be sure that the counter will not shift with use, place a line of glue around the cabinet tops before setting the marble in place. Glue marble side pieces and backsplash to the slab using a recommended adhesive. Adjust these against the wall and other counters for a tight fit.

4. Run a bead of silicone sealant around the edges, seams, and the sides of adjacent counters. With a damp rag around your finger, form a smooth concave seam. Let the sealant dry before using the counter.

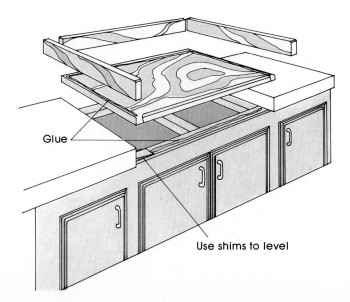

Glue

Use shims to level

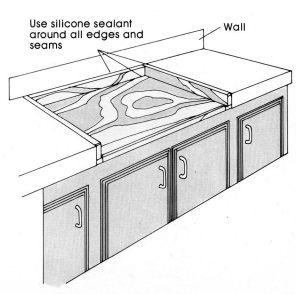

Use silicone sealant around all edges and seams

Wall

TILE COUNTER TOPS

Laying ceramic tiles on a flat counter or back wall is not difficult, but you need to plan how you want the surface to look and decide what to do with edges, corners, and spaces that are too small for full tiles. For example, you may want a drip-proof front edge or you may prefer to use wood trim for the counter's edge. If you're tiling a backsplash area, you must decide how to handle the juncture between the horizontal and vertical surfaces: A curved joint is accomplished with special cove tiles, for instance. If you want to run the tiles all the way up to the undersides of the wall cabinets, you may need to cut the top row of field tiles, but if you stop halfway, you'll probably want to use a curved-edge trim piece (bullnose tile) on the top row. Trim tiles come in many shapes and styles, and you should be aware of what is available with your particular tile. Measure the total area of counter and backsplash you want to cover, and then calculate the number of trim and field tiles you'll need. The following instructions refer to a tile counter trimmed with wood edging.

1. Starting at one end or corner of your counter, lay out the front row of field tiles, leaving space for grout lines between each tile and at the front edge. Or, if you're using trim pieces that curve at the back, start with these. Some tiles have small "ears" for grout channels. If your tiles don't, purchase a bag of tile spacers—little cross pieces—or make your own out of cardboard or rope.

2. If you don't have enough space for a full tile at the end of the first row, you have several choices: You can adjust the thickness of the grout lines; you can cut the end tile; you can push back the whole row, including grout spaces, to position the cut tile at the other end of the row; you can center the whole row and position cut tiles at both ends; or you can insert a border row of different-size tiles. The choice is an esthetic one—all the solutions work equally well. Next, lay a second row at right angles to the first. When you get to the back wall, you'll have to make the same decisions. If you want a cove tile to join the two surfaces, position that piece and then adjust your field tiles accordingly. You may have to cut the last full tile, or figure out some other solution to odd spaces. When both rows are laid out to your satisfaction, lay out all the other tiles.

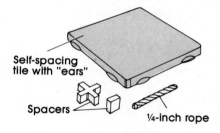

Self-spacing tile with "ears"

Spacers

¼-inch rope

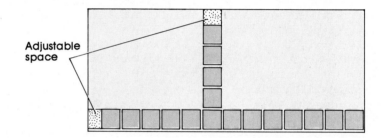

Adjustable space

Installing a Plywood Base for Ceramic Tiles

To make the base for ceramic tiles, cut ⅝-inch CDX-grade plywood to fit the tops of the base cabinets. The front-to-back depth will vary, depending on whether you want the counter to align with your drawer fronts or to hang over them. Include the thickness of a front trim tile in your calculations for the depth of your counter top (⅜ inch is normal, but your tiles may be less than ⅜ inch or you may prefer a deeper overhang). Allow for a similar overhang at any ends of the counter that don't abut a wall and at the sides and back of peninsulas and islands. Where your counter turns a corner, you'll want to lay slabs perpendicular to each other and butted tightly together. Make the cutout for the sink as shown on page 84, then position the plywood base on the cabinets, and make sure it is level and plumb. If your cabinets are level, the base should be, too. Placing it snugly against the back wall and any end walls, screw it to the base units using 1¼-inch #8 wood screws. If you are installing a recessed sink, you should do so now (see page 84). Surface-mounted sinks are installed after tiles are in place.

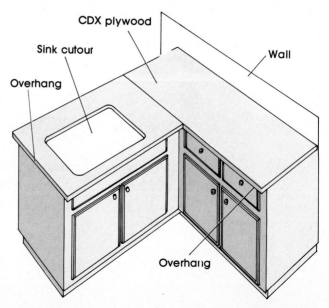

CDX plywood

Sink cutout

Overhang

Wall

Overhang

3. Lay out the backsplash/wall area. If this will consist of only one or two rows, prop one row up along the back wall and lay the other out along the last row of tiles. If you plan a higher splash wall, assemble the tiles on another surface, but make sure the backsplash tiles will align with the surface tiles. Include curved trim pieces for the top row. Lay out your wood trim strips of oak or other hardwood and mark them for cuts and mitered corners.

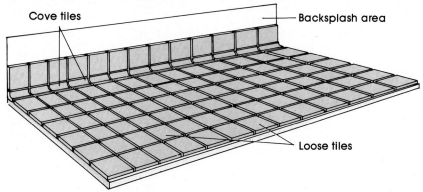

Cove tiles

Backsplash area

Loose tiles

4. When everything is laid out to your satisfaction, mark all tiles that will be cut, following the instructions in Step 6 on page 87. If you have to make a lot of cuts, rent a tile saw or take them to your tile supplier. If you have only a few cuts to make, you can score tiles with a glass cutter and snap them.

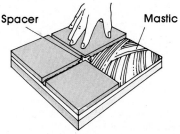

Glass cutter

Straightedge

Tile

5. Prepare the plywood base for tile installation. The type of adhesive you use depends on your tiles and base material. If you use mortar, you don't need to waterproof the plywood—just staple chicken wire over the area. If you're using wood edging, nail temporary strips to the counter edges to hold the mortar or adhesive.

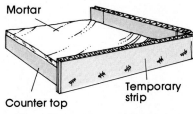

Mortar

Temporary strip

Counter top

6. Spread a layer of the appropriate adhesive over the surface with a notched trowel. Let the adhesive get tacky before laying tiles. If recommended on the package, spread a thin, ridged coating of adhesive on the back of each tile as well.

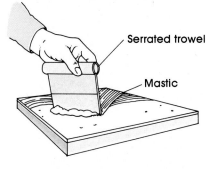

Serrated trowel

Mastic

7. Starting at one corner, gently push each tile into the mastic so it makes good contact but the adhesive does not fill the grout channels. Work away from the corner, first in one direction and then in the other. Use spacers. When all the full tiles have been laid, set in the cut or trim pieces.

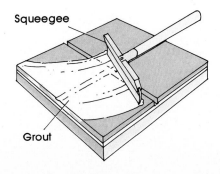

Spacer

Mastic

8. Install the backsplash tiles. Roll waterproofing on wallboard and then spread the adhesive. Starting with the row above cove tiles, spread the back of each tile with adhesive and set each firmly against the wall surface. Then set the next row, using a level to make sure it is even. Make cuts for the top row or install trim pieces.

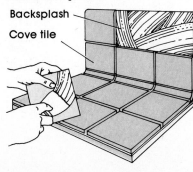

Backsplash

Cove tile

9. Remove the spacers with tweezers. Mix the grout and, with a light hand, sponge it on until all the channels are more than full and the surface is covered.

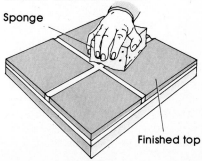

Squeegee

Grout

10. As the film dries, slowly slide a sponge or squeegee across the surface, removing some at each pass until the grout is only slightly below the tiled surface. Wait for a couple of days before installing sinks, cooktops, or wood trim. After about six weeks, seal the grout with any recommended grout sealer to keep it clean and mildew-free.

Sponge

Finished top

INSTALLING
SINKS

No matter what your counter material—tile, plastic laminate, synthetic marble, marble, or wood—surface-mounted porcelain sinks are generally installed with clamps and caulking. Self-rimming porcelain sinks need caulking only, but self-rimming stainless sinks use clamps as well. Recessed sinks are most commonly used with tile counters. Installation is similar to that of self-rimming sinks, except that the unit is set on the plywood base, not on the finished surface. Single-wall stainless sinks are not recommended for recessed installation because steel, tile, and mud have different rates of expansion and contraction. Double-wall stainless sinks may work, but porcelain and cast iron are the most common types of sinks used in recessed installations.

1. Place the sink upside down on the counter or plywood deck and position it correctly. Leave at least 1½ inches at the front edge. You can leave more if your counter is deeper than 24 inches, such as on an island or a peninsula, but don't place it farther than 2 or 3 inches back or it will be hard to reach. It probably will look best centered between the front and back edges. Draw a pencil line around the edge of the sink, then lift it off. Then draw a second pencil line ½ inch inside the first outline. Drill a hole at each corner of the inside line. It should be big enough to get your saber saw started. Using the saw, cut between the holes along the inner pencil line. Lift out the waste piece. (If you're installing a cooktop, you'll follow this same procedure—place the cooktop upside down on the counter, trace its outline or use the template supplied by the manufacturer, and center it over the base cabinet.)

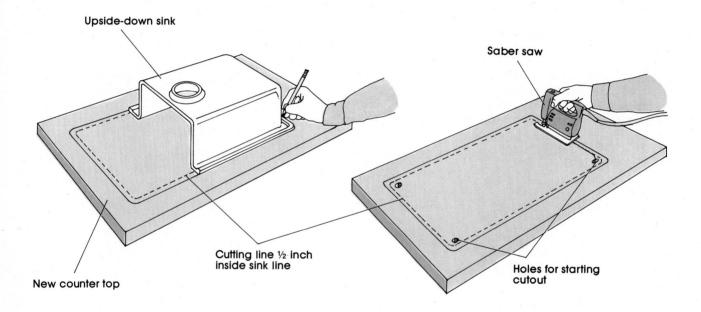

Upside-down sink

Saber saw

Cutting line ½ inch inside sink line

New counter top

Holes for starting cutout

2. Lay a bead of caulk around the bottom edge of the upside-down self-rimming sink, position it over the opening, and press down firmly until excess caulk oozes out. Attach any hardware from beneath the sink. Stainless steel sinks come with little clips that you screw tight from underneath. Heavier sinks are supported by a hanging ring that attaches to the underside of the counter top or along the edges of the cutout. Manufacturer's instructions are included with each type.

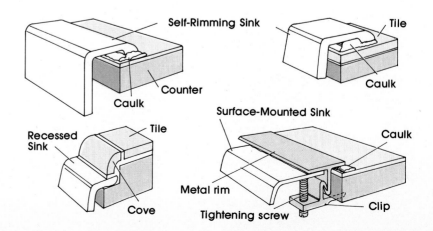

Self-Rimming Sink

Counter

Caulk

Tile

Caulk

Recessed Sink

Tile

Cove

Surface-Mounted Sink

Caulk

Metal rim

Tightening screw

Clip

FITTINGS & DISPOSALS

Once your sink is in place, you can assemble and install the faucets, connect the water supply, and hook up the drain lines. If you plan to install a tap for instant hot or cold water, you would mount it like the other faucets, following the manufacturer's directions. It should be plugged into its own 110-volt circuit, and each water device must have its own shutoff valve on the supply line.

1. Mount faucets through three of the holes in the sink or counter top; use plumber's putty. With an adjustable wrench, tighten up the hardware that holds the faucet in place. All connectors for the water supply lines can be bought as a kit, which includes the pipe (often flexible chrome tubing), all hardware shutoff valves, and installation directions. When you buy the kit, specify the diameter and material of your supply pipe. If you'll be installing a dishwasher, attach a T-shape shutoff valve (specifically designed for dishwasher connections) to the hot water supply line, and run hot water supply tubing to the dishwasher. (See page 86.)

2. Install the basket strainer by packing it with plumber's putty and pushing it firmly down into place. The strainer is threaded underneath; slip on the washer, then tighten the lock nut around the strainer collar until the basket is pulled down tightly against the basin and the putty oozes out from underneath. Clean off excess.

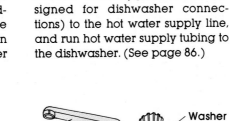
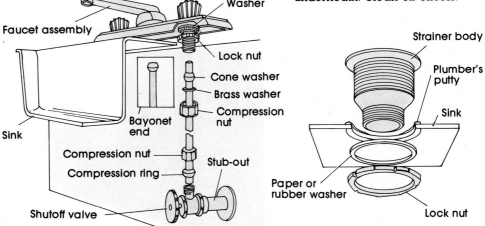

Faucet assembly
Washer
Lock nut
Cone washer
Brass washer
Compression nut
Bayonet end
Sink
Compression nut
Compression ring
Stub-out
Shutoff valve

Strainer body
Plumber's putty
Sink
Paper or rubber washer
Lock nut

3. If you're not installing a garbage disposal, install the P-trap next. Connect the tailpiece to the basket strainer, using a slip nut over a washer. Then connect the P-trap to the tailpiece with a washer and slip nut. Finally, attach the P-trap to the stub-out with a curved drain-extension pipe. Check your work carefully to make sure there are no leaks.

4. If you're installing a disposal, caulk inside the strainer portion with plumber's putty. Underneath the strainer are three screw fittings in a collar. Tighten these so the strainer is pulled tightly against the bottom of the sink. Attach the unit's tail pipe to the P or Y trap. Tighten all the fittings. Before turning on the disposal, make sure all debris is removed from inside the unit. Plug in the disposal to its own 110-volt circuit. Turn it on to test it, running the water at the same time.

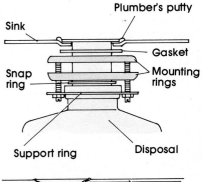

Sink
Plumber's putty
Gasket
Snap ring
Mounting rings
Support ring
Disposal

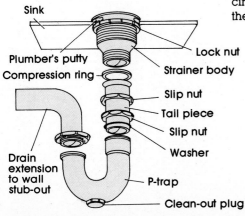

Sink
Plumber's putty
Compression ring
Lock nut
Strainer body
Slip nut
Tail piece
Slip nut
Washer
Drain extension to wall stub-out
P-trap
Clean-out plug

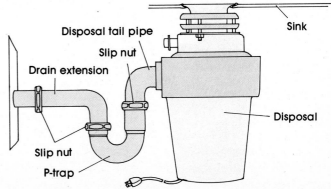

Disposal tail pipe
Slip nut
Drain extension
Sink
Slip nut
P-trap
Disposal

APPLIANCES

Some of your new, freestanding appliances will need only to be connected to their electrical outlets and pushed into place. This will be true for the freestanding range, the refrigerator with no icemaker, a separate freezer, and the trash compactor. Other appliances will require additional connections for gas, hot and/or cold water, drainage, and ducting, as well as special mounting or attachments.

Dishwashers

Dishwashers have three main connections—the black rubber drain hose, the electrical cord, and the hot water supply line. To prevent waste material from backing up into the dishwasher, an air gap is often used. The dishwasher's waste line leads up to the vent and drains into a second line leading to the disposal.

1. Drill a hole through the cabinet wall between the dishwasher and sink compartment to accommodate the three connections. Thread them through the hole, leaving a length of flexible copper tubing that will reach the dishwasher's front connections.

2. Attach the black rubber hose to the disposal by punching out the knockout on the disposal collar and fitting the drain hose to the collar with adjustable hose clamps provided. If an air gap is required, attach the dishwasher hose to the longer of the two hoses in the air gap using hose clamps. Then hook up the shorter tube from the air gap to the collar of the disposal.

3. Attach the hot-water supply line using a wrench to tighten the compression ring and nut at each end so the copper tubing fits snugly to the shutoff valve and to the fitting in front of the dishwasher.

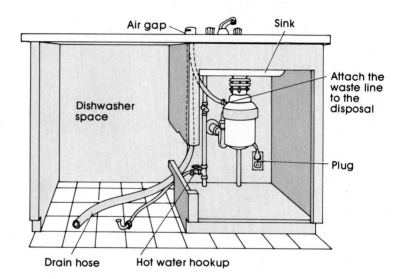

Air gap — Sink

Dishwasher space

Attach the waste line to the disposal

Plug

Drain hose — Hot water hookup

Refrigerators and Icemakers

Refrigerators are about the easiest of all appliances to install. Plug an electric one into its own 110-volt circuit and push it into place. Connect a gas unit to the flexible gas pipe that leads to the valve on the supply line. Call the gas company to check your work before you turn the gas refrigerator on. Although the refrigerator is installed after you have laid your floor, you should put in the connections for an icemaker while you are working on the sink and dishwasher.

1. Attach a T-fitting and shutoff valve on the cold-water supply line under the sink, or put a small T-tap somewhere along this line. If your refrigerator will be located some distance from the sink, run in a new cold water line or tap into another cold water line such as the one to your clothes washer or hot water heater if either is nearer.

2. Drill holes in adjoining base cabinets to accommodate the ¼-inch flexible copper pipe. Leave a large enough coil in the space for the refrigerator so it can be pulled out without being disconnected.

3. Attach a compression fitting to the end of the copper tubing and leave it until you are ready to install the refrigerator.

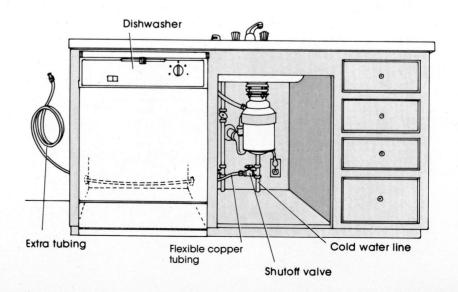

Dishwasher

Extra tubing

Flexible copper tubing

Shutoff valve

Cold water line

Hood/Vent System

A hood/vent is normally installed before the range or cooktop while it is still easy to reach the connections. The holes in the back or top of your wall cabinet should already be cut as described on page 78.

1. Connect a piece of 6- or 7-inch flexible metal ducting to the hood and to the duct pipe that enters the cabinet. If the holes are too close together for a turn, have a sheet metal box with nailing flanges built to your specifications. Make a cardboard box that fits inside the cabinet and covers both holes, mark the openings, and take it to a sheet metal worker.

2. Lift the hood into place, mark the holes for attaching it to the underside of the cabinet, drill pilot holes, and insert screws.

3. Connect the wiring. Attach the wires coming from the wall to the ones on the hood (they are usually behind the diffuser panel). Match similar colored wires and cap them. Be sure to attach the ground wire. Push the wires back into the metal receptacle, screw bulbs into the light fixtures, and replace the diffuser.

4. Connect the hood collar to the duct. This may involve wrapping silver duct tape around both or tightening a metal collar that leads to the damper. If you are using a sheet metal box, fit the venting mechanism into the box and run a bead of caulk around the flanges. Then nail them to the cabinet. Test the fan, vent, and light.

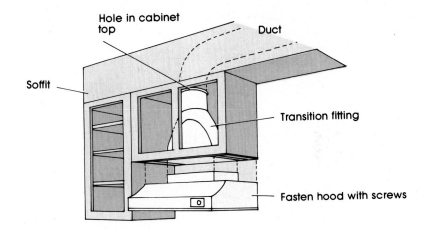

Hole in cabinet top

Duct

Soffit

Transition fitting

Fasten hood with screws

Cooktops

Commercial gas. Commercial gas cooktops sit on their own legs on top of a lowered base cabinet (which can be tiled on the top) and between base units. Steel guard strips are commonly used to protect wood or untiled cabinet edges. Connect the gas line by attaching flexible tubing to both the cooktop unit and to the gas valve, which should be located in the cabinet unit below.

Gas or electric. Cooktops designed for residential use are installed much the same as a sink, hanging through a cutout in the counter top. Follow the instructions on page 84 to remove this cutout section. Apply plumber's putty under the lip of the unit to seal it to the counter. Supplied fasteners should be tightened from below. Wire an electric unit into its own box, which should now be in the cabinet below. For a gas cooktop, connect the flexible tubing to the gas valve, which should also be in the base cabinet.

Downvent. Some cooktops are designed to direct heat and fumes down rather than up. Depending on the manufacturer, the duct is connected at the side or through the back of the cabinet. Templates for cutting the duct holes are supplied with each model. Follow the instructions on page 78 for cutting these holes and the procedures outlined above for connecting the flexible and metal ducts.

Tiled counter

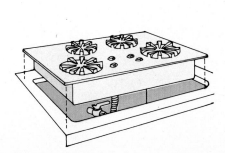

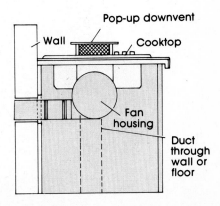

Pop-up downvent

Wall

Cooktop

Fan housing

Duct through wall or floor

Ranges and Ovens

Electric. A freestanding electric range has its own pigtail cord for plugging into a separate 220-volt circuit. To install this type of range, simply plug in the unit and slide it into place.

Gas. Hook up the gas supply line with flexible tubing, using pipe dope putty and the nuts at both ends. If your range has a pilotless ignition system, it must also be plugged into a 110-volt circuit. Call the utility company to check out your gas connections before positioning the range in its permanent position.

Drop-in. Gas and electric drop-in ranges are connected in the same manner described above, but instead of sliding into place, they are installed above a low base cabinet unit. They either hang from flanges at the counter level or are attached with screws to the base cabinet below and/or to adjacent units. To install these units, hook up the electric or gas connections and then follow the manufacturer's instructions for making the permanent attachments.

No screws

Base

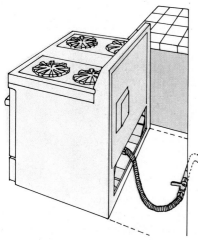
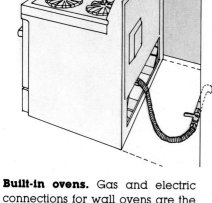

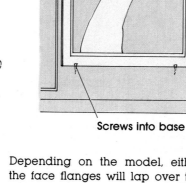

Screws into base

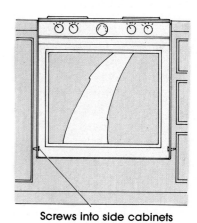

Screws into side cabinets

Built-in ovens. Gas and electric connections for wall ovens are the same as above and are usually located in an adjacent cabinet. Duct attachments for ovens are also similar to those discussed with hood/vents. To attach ovens to surrounding cabinetry, lift them into place and tighten any screw connections to the sides, top, or bottom.

Depending on the model, either the face flanges will lap over the cutout edges of the cabinet or you'll install special trim kit pieces that come with the oven or cabinet to bridge the gaps. A microwave plugs into any 110-volt circuit and may not need to be trimmed or attached.

Trash Compactor

These extremely heavy appliances are relatively easy to install. Just plug the cord into the 110-volt circuit you have provided, and then spray some soapy water on the floor to help slide it into position. Adjust any leveling legs.

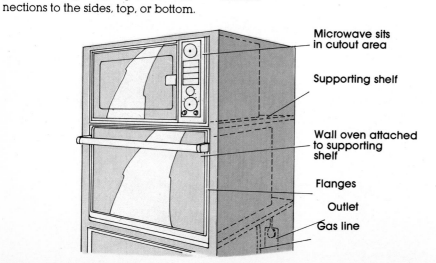

Microwave sits in cutout area

Supporting shelf

Wall oven attached to supporting shelf

Flanges

Outlet

Gas line

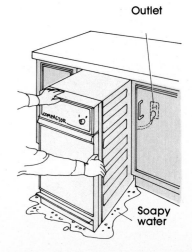

Outlet

Soapy water

LIGHT FIXTURES

Installing new light fixtures is a job that can be easily handled by even a novice do-it-yourselfer. However, the precise mounting methods vary with the individual model, so you should refer to the manufacturer's instructions. If you are changing the location of a light fixture, the new wiring should already be in place.

Standard ceiling fixtures. Unscrew the fuse or shut off the circuit breaker that powers the fixture on which you are working. If you have any doubts about whether or not the power is off, shut off all the electrical power at your service panel. Have someone hold the fixture for you while you match the wires from the light to those in the wall or ceiling. Twist similarly colored wires together and fasten them with wire caps. Attach screw mountings or thread a ceiling unit onto the central post. Slip on any face plates and screw them into place. Then turn the power back on. For more detailed instructions on installing ceiling and wall fixtures, refer to Ortho's book, *Basic Wiring Techniques*.

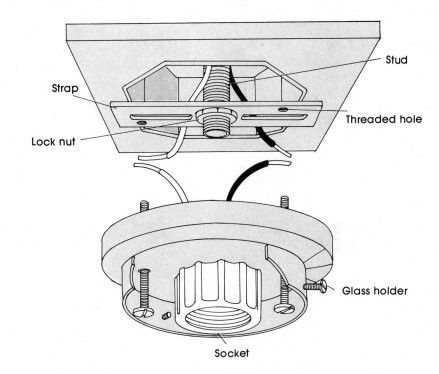

Track lights. Turn off the circuit that powers the lights you're working on. Replace the old ceiling cover with a special canopy box that is supplied with the lights. This canopy covers up the ceiling box and is grooved or slotted to accept the track. If the holes in the canopy box don't match up with those in the ceiling box, use an adaptor ring that offers several adjustable hole combinations. Attach the canopy's wires to the ceiling-box wires, capping similar colors. Screw the adaptor ring to the ceiling box, turning it this way and that until you find the right hole alignments. Then screw the canopy to the ring, possibly through a separate canopy plate if your model is not a single piece. Slide the track into the canopy box. Through each screw hole in the track, mark the ceiling with a pencil. Remove the track and drill pilot holes for toggle bolts. Put the track back into position and screw the toggles into the ceiling. Snap the light units into the track. When the connectors are in place, secure the lights with the locking levers. Position the light units so they will shed the most light on your work surfaces. Turn on the power to test where the cones of light fall. Swivel and tip the lights so that the beams fall where you want them. If the lights are too far apart or too close, slide each one along the track until the light lands where you want it. Then relock any levers that secure the units in the track.

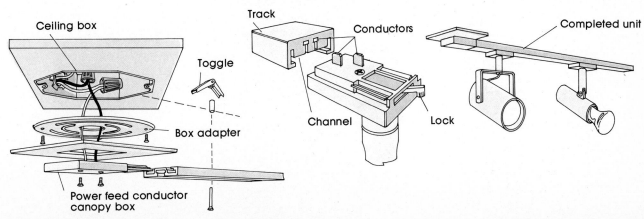

SHEET VINYL FLOORING

Because vinyl conforms to the surface beneath it, the underlayment should be very smooth. Bumps and bulges will show and could eventually damage the vinyl. Sheet vinyl requires very careful cutting, and you may prefer to let a professional do this. But if you have the patience, the procedure is relatively straightforward. Try to select a roll width that will not require butting two sheets together. If your kitchen is quite large, this may not be possible, but check out the widths available to you. The easiest way to cut your sheet to size is to unroll it in another room, and draw your kitchen layout directly on the vinyl. Then you can install it loosely or with adhesive. The loose-laid method, illustrated below, allows for subtle shifts in your walls and floor.

1. Prepare the subfloor by making sure that it is clean, smooth, and even, and that there are no protruding screws or nail heads that will pierce the new flooring. Remove any baseboards, and carefully measure your kitchen floor. Measurements around islands, peninsulas, curves, and corners should be very precise. If you're worried about accuracy, cut and tape pieces of paper together to make a pattern that entirely covers the floor.

2. Make sure the vinyl is at room temperature before working with or cutting it. Vinyl is very brittle and can snap when cold. Unroll the sheet in another room and transfer your measured outline or paper pattern to the sheet. If the vinyl has a design on it, make sure your floor pattern is straight. To protect your floor, place a thick piece of cardboard under the area you want to cut. Using a tile or utility knife and a straightedge, cut around your outline or paper pattern. Leave a few inches of extra vinyl on all sides to allow for errors. You can trim away the extra when you're installing the flooring.

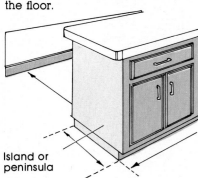

Island or peninsula

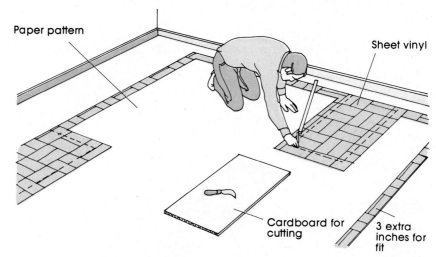

Paper pattern

Sheet vinyl

Cardboard for cutting

3 extra inches for fit

3. Take the sheet to your kitchen and position it on top of the subfloor you are covering. Make sure the design is straight, then cut around all edges so that they lay flat and come within ⅛ inch of the wall or base cabinets. This space allows for expansion and contraction of walls and floor. Molding or baseboards will cover the gap.

4. Replace or install baseboards by nailing them into the floor but not through the vinyl. Or place a piece of cardboard between the vinyl and baseboard (to make sure there is a slight gap between the two) and nail the baseboard to the wall. If you prefer, attach a matching or contrasting vinyl or rubber cove, glued to the wall. Screw on a metal threshold strip at any doorway to protect the edge of the vinyl.

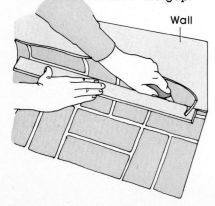

Wall

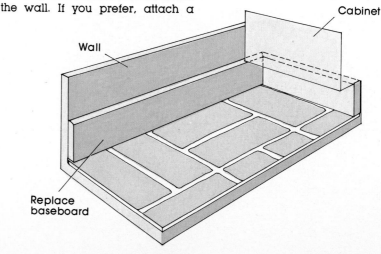

Cabinet

Wall

Replace baseboard

VINYL FLOOR TILES

Like sheet vinyl, vinyl tiles conform to the surface of the underlayment, so this surface must be free of bumps, bulges, or other irregularities. Unlike sheet vinyl, vinyl tiles are easier to install because you don't have to handle an unwieldy roll of material, and you can make tricky cuts on the spot. But tiles are slightly more expensive than sheet vinyl, and if they become loose, water can seep underneath, creating a potential rot problem. Therefore, careful installation is essential. To lay out your pattern, follow the procedure outlined in Steps 1 and 2 for Ceramic Floor Tiles (see page 92). Steps 3-6 of the ceramic floor tile instructions detail how to begin laying your tiles in one squared-off corner. Step 2 below shows you how to begin at the center of the room. Either approach will work, and you can follow the one you prefer. The idea is simply to determine where you want to place your cut tiles and then to be sure your rows are absolutely straight and even.

1. Follow Steps 1 and 2 for Ceramic Floor Tiles on page 92: Establish the center point of your kitchen, snap two chalk lines to create exact 90-degree angles, lay out two perpendicular rows of tiles to establish your pattern, and determine where you want to place cut tiles.

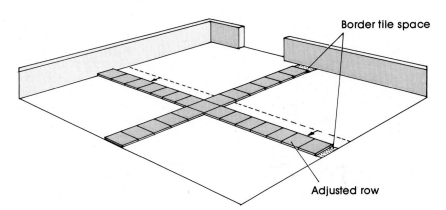

Border tile space

Adjusted row

2. When you've adjusted both rows, position your four center tiles. Using the adhesive recommended by the tile manufacturer, set these four tiles. Then, starting with the quarter of the room farthest from the door, fill in that section of the floor first. Mastics harden quickly, so cover only a small portion of the section at a time. Use only full tiles and move toward the walls in the sequence indicated. Complete each quarter of the floor in the same way as the first.

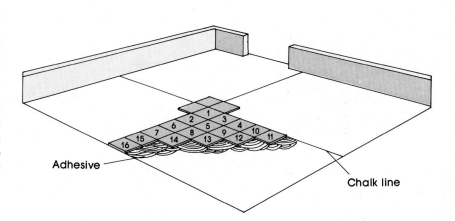

Adhesive

Chalk line

3. When all the full tiles are in place, mark, cut, and install your border tiles. To do this, turn one full tile upside down, lay it over the gap between the wall and your covered floor, and mark it where it overlaps the full tile. This will give your border tiles an exact fit with the wall. Measure and cut each border tile separately in case your wall is not straight. Then apply the adhesive and set each cut tile in place. Apply silicone seal around the bases of all cabinets and appliances. The adhesive should be dry within 24 hours, and then you can install the baseboard or molding of your choice.

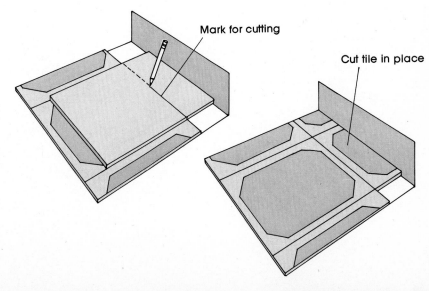

Mark for cutting

Cut tile in place

CERAMIC FLOOR TILES

Procedures for laying tiles vary for different sizes and thicknesses of tiles. Thick paver tiles are commonly set with tile adhesive on a thick bed of dry mortar. Applying a mortar bed is a job for a skilled professional—you have to work fast to smooth and level the floor before the mortar sets. Thinner, smaller tiles are commonly set over cementboard or old vinyl flooring. In these cases, you can simply spread epoxy adhesive over your patched and leveled surface. For areas that frequently get wet, spread a smooth layer of adhesive as a sealant before spreading the ridged layer. Because floor tiles are thicker than counter-top tiles, you may want to rent a commercial tile cutter if you have many cuts to make. Tile nippers will work for small trim jobs, but not for the big ones. Always wear goggles to protect your eyes when cutting tiles. Most floor tiles do not come with special trim pieces, and if you want baseboards or molding, you can choose any that seem to fit your design.

1. Starting from the center of a doorway, snap a chalk line across the kitchen, making sure that it is exactly perpendicular to the doorway. Then snap another chalk line perpendicular to the first, so the lines cross at precisely 90 degrees. Then, starting with a full tile at the doorway, lay out a row of tiles along your first chalk line, leaving space for grout between the tiles—use tile spacers.

2. When you get to the end of the line, a full tile may not fit in the remaining space. You'll have several options: Leave the row as it is and put a cut tile here, or shift the row back and put the cut tile at the doorway; shift the row to allow cut tiles of equal size at both ends; or slightly increase or decrease the width of all the grout lines. Choose the option you like best and adjust the row accordingly. Using your second chalk line as a guide, lay out another row of tiles perpendicular to the first. At the end of this row, decide where you want to place your cut tiles, and adjust the row accordingly. Then slide one of the rows over so the common tile aligns with both rows.

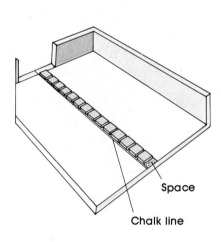

Space

Chalk line

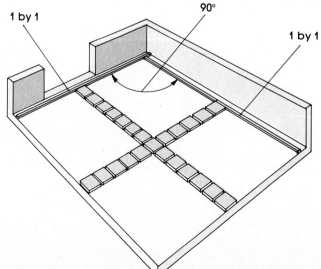

Space

Space

Space

You may have to adjust one of the two rows so they line up at the common tile

3. Next, draw a line on the floor to mark the back edge of the last full tile in one row. This line must be exactly perpendicular to the chalk line and perfectly straight even if the wall is not. Then mark the back edge of the last full tile in the other row. Draw another line the length of the room and make sure the two lines form an exact 90-degree angle at the corner. Nail down a long, straight 1 by 2 along each line, giving you a perfectly square corner from which to start laying your tiles.

1 by 1

90°

1 by 1

4. Starting in the corner, spread adhesive over an approximately 3-foot-square section, using a serrated trowel. Then gently press the corner tile into place. Inserting spacers between tiles, continue until you have finished tiling the section. Repeat this process until you have covered the floor with all the full tiles. Tamp down uneven tiles by placing a length of 2 by 4 covered with scrap carpet on the floor and tapping it gently with a mallet.

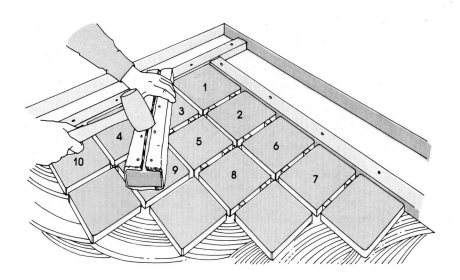

5. When the adhesive has set enough so you can walk on the floor, remove the battens and make your tile cuts. Place one tile squarely on top of the last tile in the row and another tile on top of that one. Push the top tile over the empty space, allowing for two grout lines. Using the top tile as a straightedge, draw a line across the middle tile. This is your cutting line. Measure each cut tile individually and mark them all so you'll know where each should go. Then cut all the tiles.

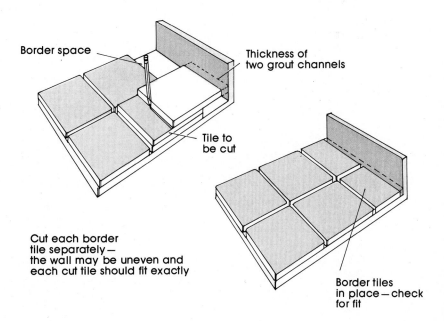

Border space

Thickness of two grout channels

Tile to be cut

Cut each border tile separately — the wall may be uneven and each cut tile should fit exactly

Border tiles in place — check for fit

6. Apply adhesive to the back of each cut tile and set it in place, leaving space for the grout lines. Allow the adhesive to set the required amount of time. Using a hard-edged window-washing squeegee, spread grout across the entire surface. Smooth the grout lines with the end of a toothbrush. Remove the excess film of grout on tile surfaces by making repeated light passes with a damp sponge until the surface is clean. Let the grout dry before walking on the floor. After several weeks, apply a grout sealer to protect against staining and mildew.

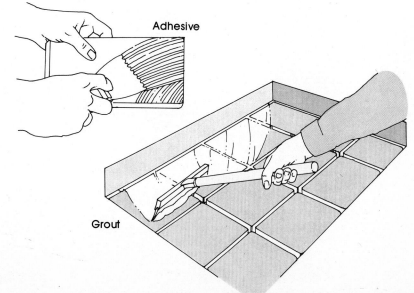

Adhesive

Grout

THE FINAL RESULT

Here is the final result of the remodeling project used as a sample throughout this book. You first saw it in its "before" stage on page 13 and then saw its plan develop on pages 42–51 as you worked out your own design. Now note the changes. On the range wall (below), light oak cabinets replace dark ones, pushing out the walls and lengthening the room with strong horizontal lines. Small blue tiles set in white grout are repeated, in reverse, in blue-on-white "graph" wallpaper. A synthetic marble slab creates an efficient baking/serving counter to the right of the range. Track fixtures beam light on work surfaces and a simple fixture lights the eating area at night. On the sink wall (far right) the refrigerator door no longer blocks dishwasher loading, and dishes can be stacked on the new stainless drainboard. At the white laminate table (right), a square clock picks up the oak wood, and natural light brightens the entire area. Much of this book was written in this cheerful spot.

Acknowledgments

Back Cover Photograph

Fred Lyon
Sausalito, CA

Photographic Locations

Diane Saeks
San Francisco, CA

Kitchen Designs and Construction

Back Cover

Metamorphosis Construction Co.
Berkeley, CA

Pages 1, 94, and 95

Marilyn Stein Gray
Designer
Hayward, CA

Gary Johnson
International Kitchen & Bath Exchange
Sunnyvale, CA

Tom Gray
Contractor
Hayward, CA

Pages 4, 32, and 33

Suzanne Brangham
Design
San Francisco, CA

Pages 11 and 16

Fordham Park Construction
El Cerrito, CA

Pages 7 and 38

Ron Silberman
Design and Construction
Fordham Park Construction
El Cerrito, CA

Front Cover and Pages 18 and 19

Kitchen of
Anthony Dias Blue
Food Writer
San Francisco, CA

Pages 20, 21, 26, 27, 28, and 29

Olivieri-Quinn Associates
Interior Design
San Francisco, CA

Pages 22, 23, and 36

Kitchen of
Loni Kuhn's Cooks Tour
San Francisco, CA

Gilbert Oliver, Architect
San Francisco, CA

Pages 30 and 31

Michael F. W. Wilson
Architect
O'Brien and Wilson Associates
Berkeley, CA

Pages 34, 35, and 36

Diane Snow Crocker
Interior Design

Page 64

Jois
San Francisco, CA

Special Thanks to:

Jois Belfield
Anthony Dias Blue
Suzanne Brangham
Peter Cully
Joan Henri
Loni Kuhn's Cooks Tour
Betsy and David Morganthaler
Maria Olivieri-Quinn
Ron and Karen Silberman
Marilyn Smith
Jim Stockton
Lu Loyola Tipping
Penny Westphal

Construction and Technical Consultants

Pat Brook
Contractor
Pleasant Hill, CA

Steve Crocker
Emminger Woodworking and Construction
Lafayette, CA

Tom Gray
Contractor
Hayward, CA

John Palmer
San Francisco, CA

Lee Zieber
Lassen Tile
Sunnyvale, CA

Interior Design Consultants

Diane Snow Crocker
Lafayette, CA

Pat Larin
Pat Larin Interiors
Los Altos, CA

Editorial Research and Assistance

Karin Shakery
Darcie Furlan
Ami Zwicker

Copyediting and Proofreading

Editcetera
Berkeley, CA

Evelyn Spire
San Francisco, CA

Graphic Design Assistants

Nancy Barbour
Mary Ann Petrillo

Illustration Assistants

Marilyn Hill
Carla Simmons

Typesetting

Lehmann Graphics
Burlingame, CA

Color Separation

Color Tech
Redwood City, CA